MW00474677

The Core of an Onion

THE
CORE
OF AN
ONION

Peeling the Rarest Common Food—
Featuring More Than 100 Historical Recipes

MARK KURLANSKY

BLOOMSBURY PUBLISHING
NEW YORK · LONDON · OXFORD · NEW DELHI · SYDNEY

BLOOMSBURY PUBLISHING
Bloomsbury Publishing Inc.
1385 Broadway, New York, NY 10018, USA

BLOOMSBURY, BLOOMSBURY PUBLISHING, and the Diana logo
are trademarks of Bloomsbury Publishing Plc

First published in the United States 2023

"To Be Hungry Is to Be Great" by William Carlos Williams, from *The
Collected Poems: Volume I*, 1909–1939, copyright ©1938 by New
Directions Publishing Corp. Reprinted by permission of New
Directions Publishing Corp.
"Ode to the Onion" from *Full Woman, Fleshly Apple, Hot Moon:
Selected Poetry of Pablo Neruda* translated by Stephen Mitchell.
Translation copyright © 1997 by Stephen Mitchell. Used
by permission of HarperCollins Publishers.
"Oda a la cebolla (Ode to the Onion)," from *Odas Elementales* © Pablo
Neruda © 1954, y Fundación Pablo Neruda
Every effort has been made to contact all copyright holders.
If notified, the publisher will be pleased to rectify any errors or
omissions at the earliest opportunity.

Bloomsbury Publishing Plc does not have any control over, or
responsibility for, any third-party websites referred to or in this book.
All internet addresses given in this book were correct at the time of
going to press. The author and publisher regret any inconvenience
caused if addresses have changed or sites have ceased to exist, but can
accept no responsibility for any such changes.

ISBN: HB: 978-1-63557-593-4; eBook: 978-1-63557-594-1

Library of Congress Cataloging-in-Publication Data is available

2 4 6 8 10 9 7 5 3 1

Typeset by Westchester Publishing Services
Printed and bound in the U.S.A.

To find out more about our authors and books visit
www.bloomsbury.com and sign up for our newsletters.

Bloomsbury books may be purchased for business or promotional use.
For information on bulk purchases please contact Macmillan
Corporate and Premium Sales Department at
specialmarkets@macmillan.com.

To Marian, unforgettable in her own way,
who never cooks but then once made me a roasted onion
in dark vinegar that I have never forgotten.
And
to the memory of Mimi Sheraton, one of the great
foodies, who advised me on this and other books.
She will be missed.

Only to have a grief
Equal to all these tears!

—ADRIENNE RICH, "PEELING ONIONS"

So consider the onion, lowly perhaps, but a thing of beauty
in itself, and certainly a gastronomic joy that should never
be taken for granted.

—JAMES BEARD, *BEARD ON FOOD*

CONTENTS

The Core of an Onion

INTRODUCTION: THE FRAGRANCE
OF THE EARTH

Onions are excellent company.

—ROBERT FARRAR CAPON,
THE SUPPER OF THE LAMB: A CULINARY REFLECTION

T hough I am bad," said the devious Grushenka, who toyed with men's hearts, "I did once give away an onion."

An onion is not a valuable thing, not even terribly nutritious, and yet if you give one to a hungry person, it could save your soul. That was Grushenka's claim, or Fyodor Dostoyevsky's in his nineteenth-century Russian masterpiece about good and evil and salvation, *The Brothers Karamazov*.

It may seem odd that Grushenka would attach that much importance to the common onion, but she was not alone. Onions have a way of taking on unexpected significance.

In much of the world, from Asia to the Mediterranean, the first step in cooking is often to chop an onion and have a good cry. Portuguese dishes often begin with cooking down chopped onions and garlic, sometimes tomatoes, in olive oil for a sauce base called *refogado*. Cooking in Tuscany often starts with a *battuto*, literally "beaten," predominantly made up of chopped onions, with some carrots, celery, garlic, parsley, and sometimes the raw bacon known as pancetta added. The Cajun food of Louisiana always begins with what is called the holy trinity— onions, celery, and peppers. In North Indian and Mughlai cuisine, all sauces begin with onions.

It may be that across the globe cooking begins with onions because once onions are sautéed, the kitchen fills with a warm, sweet, inviting fragrance that seems to promise delectable things to follow.

· · ·

In many languages, onions have served as a metaphor for the usual. In Paris slang, *Ce n'est pas mes oignons*, literally, it's not my onions—which in Parisian French sounds more like "*pas mes oignons*"—means "It's not my business."

In English, an old expression about knowing your trade was to "know your onions." Some have suggested that originally this may not have referred to onions at all but to Charles Talbut Onions, the fourth editor of the *Oxford English Dictionary*.

Canadian food writer Margaret Visser once wrote that her initial thoughts on the importance of food in shaping people and societies had come to her while she was chopping onions. "Perhaps boredom or annoyance or simply that when you chop onions, you had better keep your mind alert . . ."

Though one of the least colorful vegetables, pale next to a carrot or an eggplant, or a ripe tomato, the onion nevertheless has been recognized as a worthy still-life subject by a number of artists who excelled as colorists, including Renoir, Cezanne, and Van Gogh.

And though an onion may seem prosaic, there is probably no other vegetable that is the subject of as many poems, from those of Francisco de Quevedo, the noted seventeenth-century poet of Spain's Golden Age, who wrote of the onion with its white scarves, to the Chilean poet Pablo Neruda, who in his twentieth-century *Odes to Common Things* wrote: "The fragrance of the

Onion field on farm in 1890.

earth is alive in your crystalline nature," and "I have praised every living thing, onion. But for me you are more beautiful than a bird."

Modernist William Carlos Williams has more modest praise for spring onions (modernists are supposed to avoid extravagance):

> The small, yellow grass-onion,
> spring's first green, precursor
> to Manhattan's pavements, when
> plucked as it comes, in bunches,
> washed, split and fried in
> a pan, though inclined to be
> a little slimy, if well cooked
> and served hot on rye bread
> is to beer a perfect appetizer—
> and the best part
> of it is they grow everywhere.

Cepaphilia—a word I just made up to mean "the love of onions"—runs through history. The onion, *cepa* in botany, has detractors, but also many advocates.

Onions have always been a thing of mystery, not only because they inflict pain, but because there is an obvious and often-used metaphor in the peeling of an onion. Slowly one layer after another is removed, painfully for the peeler, though probably not for the onion.

For an onion to be appreciated, its limitations and even bad habits need to be embraced. As Robert Farrar Capon, an

American Episcopalian priest and theologian turned chef, wrote of onions, "Man's real work is to look at the things of the world and to love them for what they are." This is the story of how such a seemingly plain vegetable deemed offensive by many came to be loved for what it is.

Part One

THE WORLD ACCORDING TO ONIONS

It is hard to imagine a civilization without onions.

—JULIA CHILD

1

An Extraordinary Lily

A n onion is not a root, like a turnip or carrot, and it is certainly not a fruit. It is the bulb of a flowering plant, perhaps the most delicious of all bulbs. The bulb produced by onions, lilies, tulips, and a few other flowering plants is a ball containing the base of all the leaves. Each onion layer is the juiciest part of a leaf, storing water and carbohydrates for the next year's growth. The flowers blossom on a stalk in clusters at the top—pretty, delicate little blossoms, usually white but sometimes purple or pink, all radiating out from a common point. The flowers, if left to their own devices, become small, berry-like fruits that bear black seeds. Some varieties are grown as ornamental plants and sport a large pom-pom of pink or purple flowers.

The Dutch, the great purveyors of flowering bulbs, offer forty species of ornamental onion plants. Some bloom low to the ground and others reach four feet high, such as *Allium aflatunense* from Central Asia, with its cluster of bright pink flowers. The flowers can range from bright yellow, as with *Allium moly*, one of the more common, to the deep purple of Purple Sensation. *Allium azureum*, native to Siberia, has deep blue star-shaped flowers. *Allium giganteum*, from the Himalayas, as the name implies, has huge blossoms. The green and blue flowers are four inches wide.

The bulbs of these ornamental onions are woody and unpleasant to eat. You have to choose where the onion puts in effort, the flower or the bulb. It can't do both well. Before the flower blooms, its nutrition is stored in the bulb, but if the flower takes it, as it is supposed to do, the bulb is diminished.

In Lewis Carroll's *Alice in Wonderland*, the Queen of Hearts threatened to behead the Seven of Spades for bringing the chef a tulip bulb instead of an onion. But if the tulip has not flowered, the bulb would be good food, though not nearly as flavorful as an onion. Many flowering bulbs, such as tulips, some hyacinth, dahlias, and lilies, would be not only edible but tasty, if only the flowers were not allowed to develop. But you have to know your flowers, because some tulips and lily varieties can be poisonous. Onions are safer.

It is surprising that the onion has not received more recognition as a flower, since for a long time it was thought to belong to the lily family. But perhaps there is justice in its lack of recognition as a flower, since in more modern times, many botanists have rejected the liliness of onions and say they have their own family, *Alliaceae.*

. . .

An onion is an extraordinary lily, certainly far more talented than other lilies, which is why modern botanists don't classify them as lilies anymore. Lilies generally do not know how to defend themselves. But if the bulb of an onion is attacked, it spits back with a ferocity unmatched by other plants.

The specific type of bulb, a tunicate bulb, so called because of a variety of skin found in only a few plants and called a tunic, protects the storehouse that is the bulb. The bulb, which is connected to the soil by the roots that grow from what is called a basal plate at the bottom, stores nutrients on which the plant depends. An attack on the bulb is an attack on the most vital organ.

The farmer pulls up the bulbs when they have reached maximum plumpness, before flowers have developed to ingest the bulb's goods. At this point the papery skin is not very pronounced. But the onion must be cured, dried out, so that it will not rot. It needs a warm, dry place for curing. Ideally it lies in a sunny field. Unless it starts to rain. Rain is the curse of onion farming. Then the onions must be taken into a sheltered, airy, and warm place to dry. This is a more expensive curing and does not produce as high a quality of onion.

During the curing process the skin becomes tougher and more pronounced. In English farming folklore a thick onion skin was a predictor of bad weather, which is probably not true

Young onion field worker in Delta County, Colorado, 1939.

because by the time the thick skin has developed chances are it is too late.

Onions are perennials, plants that continue year after year. This is surprising to most people because no one lets their onions keep growing. The bulb is the key to annual regeneration—and we eat it. In that case, an onion is an annual. The bulb is harvested before the flower even begins.

Left to nature, which hardly ever happens, flowering is the ultimate goal of the bulb. After growth and flowering, the plant becomes dormant, is back at ground level, and appears to have died. For most onions this is in late spring. The bulb starts to grow again in the fall. This cycle of growth, death in spring and rebirth in fall, is the reverse of most plants.

Most farmers have sped up the process by planting previously started onions, sets, rather than seeds. Sets need a shorter growing season than onions started from seeds because the preliminary growing has already happened. Once planted the immature set will continue on its journey. Sometimes a set will "bolt," develop flowering without having produced a full bulb. This is why farmers buy sets commercially that have been heat treated to prevent bolting.

A farmer could keep some plants for seeds but this would mean losing out on those bulbs and the seeds would be of inconsistent quality. A good seed company tries to guarantee all its seeds.

Depending on the climate, an onion field can have two or three harvests. But it does make demands on the soil and the field needs to be periodically rotated with other crops. Certain crops, such as tomatoes, do especially well planted with onions. This is why onions and tomatoes are a traditional mix in many cultures.

Although a hearty crop, onions are subject to certain diseases. Fungi are a problem. Downy mildew attacks in cool moist regions such as in Northern Europe. A mildew called white rot is also a problem in northern fields. Onion smut is a deadly blight to most of the onion family. Neck rot attacks onions while in storage, especially if the storage place is too moist. There are also bacteria, such as soft rot, and a variety of viruses that can attack onions.

Many of these illnesses can be avoided in a dry climate; but then there are insects to worry about such as the onion thrip that drills a hole in the leaf and sucks out sap or the onion fly, whose larvae, known as onion maggots, eat onions.

. . .

Onions are mild unless attacked. Most do not even have a strong smell. But bitten or cut, they retaliate. The toxic spittle the vengeful onion sends into your eyes is low-molecular-weight substances with sulfur atoms, which is an extremely rare way for chemicals to present themselves in nature. It is said that they are spewing sulfur. But to say that is to ignore the unusual complexity of the operation. The molecules are "highly reactive"; in other words, they change very easily. One sulfur compound becomes a different one, which can then become a different one so they can do a number of things. The most famous, the one we care about, is that they become *lacrimatory*; they induce tears, make you cry. The molecules dissolve into the water of the eyes and turn into sulfuric acid, a nasty little trick designed for defense. Onions are designed to fight against mammals.

The compound activates nerve endings in the cornea that send a message to the brain translated as pain. The purpose of all pain messages is to tell you to stop whatever is causing it. It teaches most animals to stay away but humans are undeterred.

This sulfur compound, propanethial-S-oxide, a form of sulfur oxide, is completely different from the compound that gives the onion its smell and strong taste. You smell the onion as you feel the sting so it seems to be the same thing, but it is not. The smell of onions does not hurt your eyes. The pain comes from that odorless lacrimator, that tear inducer. An entirely different set of compounds with unstable sulfonic acids combine with ammonia and pyruvic acid to produce the pungent flavor and smell. Once it has been ingested, this sulfur compound will try to escape through expiration and perspiration and causes unpleasant breath and sometimes body odor.

But because the sulfur compounds are so unstable, they do not hang out for long. They are easily transformed. Heat, for example, completely changes them, which is why a cooked onion does not taste or smell or act anything like a raw onion. The new compound can be more than fifty times sweeter than table sugar. This transformation from the harsh raw onion is probably why there have always been so many recipes for baking, stewing, and roasting whole onions throughout the centuries. There has been a sense that onions are a tough and harsh thing that needs to be tamed, that they cause pain but are worth it, that, in the words of Pablo Neruda, they make you "weep without suffering."

These compounds that cause pain or give off strong odors or flavor, the traits for which the onion is famous, are not vital to the life of an onion. They are extravagant extras, what is known in botany as a secondary metabolite. Primary metabolites are ones that are necessary for growth, development, or reproduction. But this secondary chemistry is only useful for defense. It also does attract pollinators, which aids in reproduction, but even this is not vital to the life of an onion because they are capable of self-pollination.

In botany an onion is known as genus *Allium*. One of the most numerous plant genera, there are between 600 and 750 different species of *Allium*. In their class, *Monocotyledons*, one of two classes of flowering plants, only the orchid genus has more species. The word *allium* may come from a Celtic word meaning "strong flavored." Others say it is from the Greek *aleo*, "to avoid," because of the pungency. The Celtic version is more pleasant but the Greek more likely.

Many species are considered weeds and most are edible and have been eaten by locals where they grow wild. Only about a dozen have been cultivated for food. A few are loved by gardeners for their flowering beauty though sometimes these are rejected because they are so strong smelling. Odiferous sulfur compounds are a characteristic of the genus.

When the name was first given in 1753 by Carl Linnaeus, who established the naming system for the natural order, he described only thirty species. New ones are being discovered regularly. This book is concerned with the species *Allium cepa*, onions, although *Allium sativum*, garlic, is credited with many of the same miraculous qualities and the same negatives: bad breath and unpleasant odors.

Onion recipes throughout the centuries have offered a variety of strategies to ease the pain or even avoid tearing. A Chinese text from the Song dynasty (960–1279) recommended ginger and jujubes, sometimes called Chinese dates. The parsley cure for both breath and tearing eyes was suggested in 1629 by London apothecary John Parkinson in his *Paradisi in Sole*, which also prescribed onion juice to heal burns.

Florence Irwin, an early 1900s traveling Irish "domestic science" instructor, taught her students to remove the sting from onions by a technique called scalding. This was her technique, which actually works:

Soldier peeling onions with an anti-onion gas mask at Camp Kearny, California, 1917–1919.

> Peel the onions, place in a basin, add a pinch of salt.
> Cover with fast boiling water. Leave about one minute.
> Strain off the water.

Some suggest that the pain to the eyes can be reduced by running water near them. This seems a folk cure, but it has a scientific underpinning: just as the sulfur compound is drawn to the water of the eyes, it will be drawn away to the tap water. Keeping onions cold in the refrigerator can also help, because cold reduces the onion's ability to release its gases. Using a sharp knife is a good idea, because the sharper the knife, the fewer cells are disturbed, but the onion can still make you cry. It is sometimes suggested that lighting a match, holding an unlit match in your teeth, holding a crust of bread in the mouth, or biting on the handle of a wooden spoon can help. There is not much science behind those solutions. I have found some success with the running water or refrigeration, and none with the bread, match, or wooden spoon. Something that I have found helpful that, oddly, is rarely mentioned, is to protect your eyes by wearing glasses. Onion goggles are available too. But if the compound can get to your nose, it has a pathway to your eyes.

· · ·

Onions are a tough breed, prospering in sandy or stony ground where they do not have many competitors. Wild onions thrive in the arid Middle East, tropical Africa, and northern Europe. But there is a terroir element to onion growing. The same variety will turn out differently in different soil and different climate. The amount of sulfur in the soil, or even the air, determines how pungent the onions will be. Hot climates produce a denser, less juicy, and more pungent onion than milder climates. This is one of the reasons why Indian food in London and New York is not the same as in India. The hot Indian climate produces a tougher, more pungent onion.

· · ·

The name *onion* comes from the Latin word *union*, which means single, because an onion has a single bulb as opposed to garlic and other relatives that have clusters of bulbs. Romans called onions *unionem*. From there it became *unyon* in Middle English, then *onion* or, in French, *oignon*.

Other members of the *Allium* family include not only garlic and *Allium schoenoprasum*, which are chives, but also *Allium ampeloprasum*, or elephant garlic, and *Allium tuberosum*, otherwise known as Chinese or garlic chives. *Allium schoenoprasum*, chives, are perhaps the smallest, least imposing looking onion, but they are one of the toughest. They withstand heat and drought but also flourish in frozen northern tundra in Alaska and Siberia.

Allium porrum, which are leeks, are planted in six-inch-deep furrows that are gradually filled in as the leek grows so that the lower part remains white. Similar species include *Allium kurrat*, which are a Middle Eastern leek, and *Allium fistulosum*, which are Japanese bunching onions. Another family member, *Allium victorialis*, is known as *gyoja ninniku* in northern Japan.

Most of the alliums known in the West seem to have originated in Central Asia and later found their way into China. But there are Chinese originals including bunching onions, *Allium chinense*, which is commonly pickled and eaten as a snack in China; the Chinese leek, *A. ramosum*; Chinese garlic, *A. macrostemon*; a small onion, *A. ledebourianum*; and *A. tuberosum*, known in Chinese as *chiu-ts'ai*. Some botanists also believe that the cultivated garlic of China and Japan are derived from native species.

Ramps, *Allium tricoccum*, grow wild in North America as do *Allium ursinum*, the strong-smelling ramsom, or ramson. The Irish have a centuries-old tradition of placing strips of wild ramsom found in the woods in shoes to help with colds or coughs. Ramsom also commonly grow wild throughout Europe and traditionally were fed to young hens as an inducement to start laying eggs, a folk measure with little science behind it.

Shallots, *Allium ascalonicum*, are sometimes added to this list. Greeks and Romans thought that they originated in Ascalon, or Askelon, on the Israeli coast below Tel Aviv. This might have been a trading point rather than the site of the fields. The word *scallion* has the same origin and scallions, green onions, and spring onions are all different cepae. A scallion is an onion pulled from the ground when still very immature.

In the southern United States, shallots, which, despite tolerating winter well, prefer warm, humid climates, are often called scallions. Tree onions, sometimes called Egyptian onions, though they are not from Egypt, have small bulbs and grow two-foot-high stems.

.   .   .

For thousands of years learned people have argued whether onions were a healthy or unhealthy food. A 600 B.C.E. medical text recommends that religious people such as Brahmins and Hindu widows avoid onions in their quest for deeper spirituality. Onions and garlic, like pork, mushrooms, and a few other foods, were said to be *tama*, literally containing the quality of darkness. Such tama foods were said to lead to ignorance, sloth, lewdness, and fear in those who ate them. And yet Susruta also writes in the *Susruta Sushruta* that onions are healthy for digestion, eyesight, joints, and a healthy heart. The manuscript suggested that religious people feed onions to cows and drink the milk and in that way they could enjoy the health benefits of forbidden alliums without ingesting them.

In Chinese Buddhist culture there is a list of five vegetables not to be eaten because of their strong odor. They are all alliums, although sometimes ginger is included. These foods supposedly led to sexual desire and bad temperament. The idea of the five banned strong-smelling vegetables spread in China to Taoism and other religions. But the Chinese, going back to ancient times, have tried to fight fevers, cholera, and dysentery with onion tea.

The ancient Egyptians saw the concentric layers of an onion as a metaphor for the structure of the universe. Onions were painted on the walls of pyramids and tombs, perhaps as a symbol of eternal life, evoked by the sphere within a sphere within a sphere structure of the onion.

Onions were placed in the bodies or by the head of mummies, or tied to the feet or along the legs. Ramses IV, who reigned for only about six years and died in 1150 B.C.E., had onions placed in his eye sockets. Egyptologists argue about the meaning of these funereal onions. Some think the Egyptians believed the strong smell and taste of onions could awaken the dead. But it is also possible that they thought onions would help preserve the mummies.

The circa 1550 B.C.E. Egyptian religious book known as the Ebers Papyrus contains numerous therapeutic uses of onion and garlic. In the second century B.C.E., a formula for a magic spell was recorded that consisted of salt, doe fat, mastic, myrtle, dark bay, barley, crab claws, sage, rose, fruit pits, fig, a dog-faced baboon's dung, the egg of a young ibis, a single onion, and garlic.

But onions always have a downside. The first-century-C.E. Greek biographer Plutarch wrote that in ancient Egypt, "The priests keep clear of the onion and detest it and are careful to avoid it because it is the only plant that naturally thrives and flourishes in a waning moon. It is suitable for neither fasting nor festival because in the one case it causes thirst and in the other tears for those who partake of it."

Some Greeks, though, thought onions had positive powers. In Homer's *Odyssey*, Odysseus calls on the power of onions to gain him entry to Circe's lair. A few centuries later, Hippocrates, considered the father of medicine, prescribed onions to prevent pneumonia, as a diuretic, and for healing wounds.

The Olympic athletes of ancient Greece prepared for their contests by eating onions, either for strength and power or for good fortune. An athlete might eat a pound of onions and also drink onion juice, and rub onion on his body. This must have made a strong impression on opponents.

Alexander the Great had his armies eat onions because he thought their strong flavor signaled that they would make his troops strong. Dioscorides, a first-century-C.E. physician who served the military under the Roman emperor Nero, believed in medical uses for onions, garlic, and leeks.

At the same time, Pliny the Elder listed twenty-seven different remedies using onions, sixty-one with garlic, and thirty-nine with leeks. He believed onions could cure bad vision, cure insomnia, heal mouth sores, relieve toothaches, and cure dysentery. "Importance has recently been given to chives by the emperor Nero," he wrote, "who on certain fixed days of every month always ate chives preserved in oil and nothing else, not even bread, for the sake of his voice."

. . .

Onions were often avoided because of an association with meat. In India, the Hindu Baniya cult banned the eating of onions because some onions are red, and all red food was forbidden because it resembled meat. Some sects in China rejected the eating of onions because their strong flavor resembled that of meat. In Europe, the medieval Church banned the eating of onions on holy days because their strong flavor classified them as a hot food, like meat, as opposed to other vegetables that were mild-tasting and considered cold.

Religion aside, being a warm rather than cool food was sometimes seen as having advantages. An eleventh-century Arab medical treatise that somehow ended up in Europe with a Latin title, *Tacuinum sanitatis* ("Maintenance of Health"), stated, "The onion is excellent and highly suitable for old people and those with cold temperaments, because of its nature which is warm in the highest degree, sometimes moist and sometimes dry." Bartolomeo Sacchi, born in the village of Piadena near Cremona in 1421, became one of the most celebrated authorities on health in the Italian Renaissance, under the name Platina, which is Latin for Piadena. In his book *On Right Pleasure and Good Health*, published in 1465, he wrote:

> About onions, doctors agree for the most part that inflammations are clearly kindled by them, the head made to

ache, brain and memory impaired, deep sleep induced, phlegmatic humors sometimes generated and other times removed. Some, however, think they are healthful when used moderately because they soften the bowels, induce dreams, create appetite, especially arouse sexual appetite and increase its foment with lustful dampness.

In medieval Europe preventing hair loss was added to the benefits of onions. Giacomo Castelvetro, a seventeenth-century Italian refugee who tried to improve British diets, claimed that onions were "excellent for clearing up the sort of bad cough that lingers after a cold."

And of course, with all this, how could onions fail to be labeled an aphrodisiac. Apicius, the first-century-c.e. Roman gourmet, quoted Marcus Terentius Varro, Roman scholar of two generations earlier, as saying that if they are cooked in water, onions will lead to love—the exact phrase being *"qui Veneris ostium quærunt,"* "seek the mouth of Venus"—and consequently should be served at weddings.

The German Dominican monk Albertus Magnus (1193–1280), who considered himself an agronomist and scientist, did not include onions in his list of suitable garden plants. Both garlic and leeks made the list. His exclusion of onions, which are not any more difficult to cultivate than garlic and leeks, may be tied to his discovery that onions were an aid in fertility, increasing male sperm and the lactation of mothers. Onions were always seen as a potent herb perhaps just because they tasted so potent.

In the twelfth century the Berber Umar Ibn Mohammed Al Nefzawi wrote *The Perfumed Garden*. While Europe was in its dark ages, books flourished in the Arab world and this became the leading work on sex. Perhaps it was too successful, promoting inappropriate behavior. He later said, "I did wrong to put this book together."

One of the important tips from *The Perfumed Garden* was to increase virility by drinking onion juice and honey. Other onion formulas were suggested to increase performance. In France, not surprisingly, onion soup was credited with this gift. Onion juice, ghee, and honey with a milk chaser is the great natural aphrodisiac in India. Jainists, Brahmans, and some Chinese Buddhist priests rejected onions because their heat could lead to sexual excitement. This is also why the Catholic Church banned onions on holy days.

When the city of Pompeii was excavated after being destroyed by a volcanic eruption, the charred remains of onions were preserved in lava in what had been the brothel.

Onions were often used for sexual innuendos. A 975 C.E. Anglo-Saxon text, *The Exeter Book*, or *Codex exoniensis*, contained in addition to stories nearly one hundred riddles or enigmata, a dozen of which seem to have sexual references. But in reality they are about something more mundane. Riddle number 25 is:

> I am a wondrous creature: to women a thing of joyful expectation, to close-lying companions serviceable. I harm no city-dweller excepting my slayer alone. My stem is erect and tall—I stand up in bed—and whiskery somewhere down below. Sometimes a countryman's quite comely daughter will venture, bumptious girl, to get a grip on me. She assaults my red self and seizes my

Mexican workers in San Fernando Valley pulling up sets from a seedbed to transplant to an onion field, 1930.

head and clenches me in a cramped place. She will soon feel the effect of her encounter with me, this curl-locked woman who squeezes me. Her eye will be wet.

The book did not answer the riddles but the solutions were not what they seemed. So while riddle 25 appears to be referring to a male sex organ, scholars have determined that it is a reference to an onion, or *ynioleac* in Anglo-Saxon.

. . .

Onions were often credited with nutritious value. The seventh-century Benedictine monk in Northumbria known as the Venerable Bede wrote in Latin a biography of Saint Cuthbert, a contemporary Northumbrian monk. Cuthbert was a hermit and, according to Bede, spent five days in a place with no food supply. Cuthbert was asked, "Surely you have not stayed in one place so long without taking food?" He pulled back a cover—here we picture a saintly smile—and showed five onions and said, "This was my food these five days for as often as my mouth was parched and burned through excess of dryness and thirst, I sought to refresh and cool myself by tasting these." It was found that less than half of only one of the onions had been "nibbled away." Well, don't try this at home. Not much nutrition for five days.

Marco Polo reported that the people of Hormuz ate nothing but salted tuna and onions and were very healthy. Tuna was probably pivotal to this meager diet.

In the late Middle Ages it came to be understood that onions were rich in vitamins that were badly lacking in European diets. But also they stored well and were one of the few foods that easily kept through the winter.

Seventeenth- and eighteenth-century merchant sailors, plagued by scurvy on long voyages, found that onions, which stored well on ships, prevented this disease that was caused by a lack of vitamins, and so onions became a standard ship provision.

Mistress Margaret Dods, in her influential 1829 book, *The Cook and Housewife's Manual*, wrote that raw onions "form the favorite *bon-bons* of the [Scottish] highlander who, 'with a few of these and an oat-cake,' says Sir John Sinclair, 'would travel an incredible distance and live for days without other food.'"

Mistress Dods existed, however, only in the pages of a Walter Scott novel, *St Ronan's Well*. The real cookbook author was an early feminist writer, journalist, and novelist in Edinburgh, Christian Isobel Johnstone.

Fannie Merritt Farmer, who became a food guru of working women from her perch as principal of the Boston Cooking School, said of onions in her 1896 book, "They are wholesome, and contain considerable nutrients, but are objectionable on account of the strong odor they impart to the breath." The novelist and opinion columnist Mary Virginia Hawes Terhune, a.k.a. Marion Harland, went even further, writing of onions, "No more nutritious vegetable ever finds its way to our table." This, of course, is untrue, but there are so many more reasons for onions to find their way to our table.

. . .

The most persistent criticism of onions, even more than the sting, is that the chemicals that they release cause bad breath. Ancient Greeks banned onion eaters from the sacred temple of the goddess Cybele because of their breath. Surprisingly, onion breath jokes never got old. The first-century Roman poet Martial wrote:

> He who bears chives on his breath
> Is safe from being kissed to death.

In Shakespeare's *A Midsummer Night's Dream*, while the theater company is preparing to stage a comedy, Bottom cautions the actors not to eat onions, so that the comedy will have sweet breath. On the other hand, in *The Taming of the Shrew*, a boy about to take on the role of a wife given to tears is advised to use onions to manufacture weeping.

In Cervantes's *Don Quixote de la Mancha*, Don Quixote wisely counsels his peasant vassal, "Eat not garlic nor onions, lest they find out thy boorish origins by the smell."

A fourteenth-century Arab recipe collection, *Kitâb Wasf al-Atima al-Mutada* ("The Description of Familiar Foods"), is concerned about the smell of the cook who has been handling onions and recommends, "Wash your hand before ladling, and perfume it against the smell of onions."

Marion Harland, in an enormously popular cookbook, *Common Sense in the Household*, published in 1871, said that onion breath could be cured by "chewing and swallowing a few grains of roasted coffee."

It is often suggested that eating parsley cures onion breath, though this has been debunked. Kiwifruit and eggplant have also been proposed. None of these cures has been scientifically proved, however.

There are communities in the United States that still have old ordinances on their books against eating onions in public places, especially movie theaters. Texas A&M University researched and found numerous examples, though they are almost never enforced and most of these communities are not even aware that such ordinances exist. Some are too bizarre to explain. In Ridgeland, South Carolina, a woman weighing more than two hundred pounds cannot be seen eating onions in a restaurant or at a public picnic if she is wearing shorts. It is illegal to eat onions while

walking down the street in Northfield, Connecticut. In Dyers-
burg, Tennessee, it is illegal to enter a movie theater within four
hours of having eaten an onion. In Nacogdoches, Texas, there
is an ordinance against "young women" eating raw onions, on
burgers or otherwise, after six P.M. These forgotten ordinances do
suggest that eating raw onions, which they indicate is especially
inappropriate for women, was more popular than may be
supposed. Otherwise, why have the ordinance?

In fact, the habit of eating raw onions, though often dispar-
aged because of the odor, has been popular in different cultures
throughout history. In the year 972, a Muslim merchant visiting
the island of Sicily, then part of the Arab Empire, was struck
by the quantity of onions in the city of Palermo and appalled by
the local habit of eating them raw. He wrote in 974 of Sicilians:

> They eat it at home, morning and evening, among
> all their classes so it spoiled their imagination and
> damaged their brains and confused their senses and
> changed their minds and lessened their understanding
> and discolored their faces.

Worth the risk, raw onion was popular in medieval salads
and both the Sicilians and the British in the Middle Ages would
simply hold an onion in the hand and eat it like an apple.

Jonathan Swift warned against eating onions raw:

> There is in every cook's opinion,
> No savoury dish without an onion:

> But lest your kissing should be spoiled
> The onion must be thoroughly boiled.

In many societies, including in seventeenth-century England, eating onions raw came to be thought of as a lower-class taste associated with peasants. Peasants smelled oniony. Jean Baptiste Bruyerin, a sixteenth-century doctor from Lyon, wrote that onions "are eaten raw by rather refined people, the more polished nonetheless prefer them cooked more, first of all because they are healthier that way and also because they do not give off such a strong odor."

John Evelyn, in his 1699 *Acetaria: A Discourse of Sallets* (salads), allowed that raw onions were "more proper for our Northern Rustics." The sixteenth-century English derided the Scots for smelling of raw onions: "They nauseate the very aire with their tainted breath, so perfumed with onions, that to an Englishman it is almost infectious," reported an English traveler in Scotland.

In India in the time of the Mughals, a Muslim empire from the sixteenth to the nineteenth century, poor Muslims ate raw onion with rice and aristocratic Muslims only ate cooked onions. In more recent times, snacking on raw onions has been particularly popular in central Europe. The great Albanian novelist Ismaïl Kadaré describes a typical peasant breakfast as corn bread, cheese, and raw onion.

Taking a train through what was then Yugoslavia in the 1970s, I often saw people snacking on onions like fruit. It is common in the Balkans, Romania, and many other parts of the region. I asked a Polish friend if people ate onions like that in Poland. "Oh no," he sneered. "The Russians and the Ukrainians, but not the Polish." Then he thought for a moment and added, "Except for my crazy cousin. I will be cooking something and have the food laid out in the kitchen. When it is time for the onion, it is gone. Then I see my cousin over in the corner, munching away. He is crazy."

The late James Beard, one of the greatest American food writers, not only loved onions; from an early age he loved them raw too. "I crawled into the vegetable bin, settled on a giant onion and ate it, skin and all. It must have marked me for life for I have never ceased to love the hearty flavor of onions."

.   .   .

A few benefits are agreed on. Onions, though not as nutritious as some high-protein food, have a great deal of vitamin C and also contain calcium and iron. They are low on sodium and have no fat. An onion is only about 45 calories, sometimes less. But they are about 89 percent water, which is slightly more than people.

Many claims about onions remain unproven, such as their supposed cancer-fighting properties, or that they reduce blood sugar, relieve asthma, cure cholera, heal goiters, reduce hiccups, relieve jaundice, reduce the risk of osteoporosis. Onions fried in ghee is an Indian remedy for acne. Smell onion juice to stop a nosebleed. Onion juice mixed with honey fights off flu. Onions boiled in molasses are said to help a sore throat. Pliny's claim that onions ease insomnia has persisted, and folk medicine still suggests eating an onion before going to bed. One British guide even suggested eating "two or three onions" before retiring.

.   .   .

Alliums can kill insects, which is sometimes useful, but they can also damage the blood of cats and dogs. Pets should never be fed onions or garlic—or most other bulbs.

Onions have an ability to stave off some bacteria (which might have been helpful in preserving mummies). Louis Pasteur believed onions had this property. So did Albert Schweitzer, fighting off amebic dysentery in Africa, though Schweitzer seemed to prefer using garlic. Onions became a basic provision of the U.S. Army, not only as food that would not easily spoil, but to help heal wounds. In the height of the Civil War, commanding Union general Ulysses Grant found himself with insufficient onion provisions and sent a message to the War Department saying, "I will not move my troops without onions." He was sent three wagonloads of them, according to legend, the following day.

The use of onions when antiseptics were not available, to prevent infections in wounds, continued. In World War II the Russian Red Army sometimes resorted to onions for wounds.

Before bacteria was fully understood, anything that seemed to fight off infection was thought to chase away evil. Bram Stoker, in his 1897 *Dracula*, showed garlic being used to drive off a vampire, and this stems from an older myth that both garlic and onions drive off evil spirits.

Palestinians sometimes arrive at protests with an onion, which some believe can protect them from Israeli tear gas. The theory is that a natural tear-producing organism would steal the fire from an artificial one. It doesn't work.

Onions have inspired the imagination of many to believe they hold almost magical powers to cure almost anything, but actually their powers lie elsewhere.

2

Old World Onions

I t seems that it is human nature to dig up wild onion bulbs and eat them. They look succulent, have an enticing scent, and announce themselves as food. It is not known for how long people have been doing this, though it seems certain that even in prehistoric times before agriculture became well established, people living on wild plants dug up and ate a variety of bulbs. The bulbs are easy to find because of the flowers on top. Traces of onion bulbs along with fig seeds and date pits have been found in Jericho in the Jordan Valley dating back to 5000 B.C.E.

Someone at some point dug up bulbs of the wild species, planted them, fussed over them in a garden, and produced an even more edible plant, probably resulting in a bigger, juicier bulb.

Even the ancient Romans ate hyacinth, gladiola, lily, and asphodel bulbs, probably cultivating them like onions and harvesting them before flowering to maintain the quality of the bulb.

The best of the bulbs sampled by early humans were probably wild forebearers of the onion. We know that wild onions, left to their own devices, grow on stony, unpromising ground. These perennials struggle on for years before flowering.

The wild forbearer of the *Allium cepa* is thought to have first been cultivated in Iran or West Pakistan, Tajikistan, Uzbekistan, or Turkmenistan, but this is only a guess, since no wild cepae exist there or anywhere else anymore. Similar species have survived in the wild in this area. But they may have been everywhere—all six continents. They have probably been cultivated for five thousand years, since the origin of agriculture. This is because they are easy to grow, will grow in many climates and soils, and, once harvested, are easy to store.

Since there are no wild cepa onions left anywhere in the world, it is not certain what this wild plant that led farmers to grow domestic ones was like. Even 2,000 years ago, Pliny the Elder wrote, *"Cepea silvestesa no sun"*—"There are no wild onions." This unusual absence of ancestry suggests that the cepa may have been one of the first plants to have been cultivated, one of humankind's first crops.

Onions are thought to descend from one of the many wild alliums that still grow in Asia, but it is not certain which of them. The leading suspects are *Allium oschaninii*, or *Allium praemixtum*, which are closely related and still found wild in Central Asia, or *Allium vavilovii* from Kopet in the Dagh Mountains of Turkmenistan, or *Allium pskemense*, which grows wild in the

Pamir Mountains of western Tibet, where the bulbs are gathered, transplanted, and cultivated to have much larger, singular bulbs, to be used for both food and medicine. These wild onions are all near extinction from being overharvested for food. Another possibility is *Allium galanthum*, sometimes called the snowdrop onion, which grows in Kazakhstan, Mongolia, and the Tien Shan Mountains. All of these have small bulbs and hollow leaves that swell to a thickness halfway up. They all have an oniony scent and contain allicins—alkyl sulfides—that sting the eyes. The ancient farmers who developed this species must have wanted to keep or even emphasize this trait, to keep animals from eating their crop.

If we knew what the ancestor was, we would know what aspects of *A. cepa* were designed by humans, just as we have to study wolves to completely understand dogs. We do not know what characteristics they aimed to emphasize and which they aimed to reject. We can only suppose that they ended up with what they wanted, which would make onions one of the first foods of human design.

During the Han dynasty, a period of great flowering of Chinese culture from about 206 B.C.E. to 210 C.E., *A. cepa* became popular in China. They may have arrived earlier, but the fact that they were called *hu-t'sung*, "foreign onions," and still are, indicates that either the bulbs or the seeds were introduced from somewhere else, most likely India. The Chinese had other species of onions that were native, however, including shallots, both red and white. White shallots were considered superior.

The Chinese have always had a preference for the Welsh onion, which was thought to have warming properties and was recommended for winter weather. The Welsh onion, *Allium fistu-losum*, has never been from Wales. Its origin is Asian and it is also called a bunching onion, sometimes a Japanese bunching onion, a green onion, or a spring onion. Bunching onions resemble scallions in appearance but are much milder in flavor. Substituting scallions for bunching onions is one of the reasons Chinese food in the West tastes different than in China. The name *Welsh onion* comes from German, though the Germans are not nearly as associated with it as the Chinese and Japanese. The Germans acknowledge this, which is why they called it *welsche*, which means "foreign"—a foreign onion.

The Welsh onion dominates Chinese cooking and in the north is the primary vegetable along with a native leek, slightly different from the Western variety. Only as Western items have started to find their way into Chinese life has there been an increased use of the *Allium cepa* bulb.

In a traditional Chinese meal, each of the numerous dishes has its place on the table. As the table is set, meat that is cooked on the bone is always placed on the left, and sliced meat on the right. Some dishes are placed on the outside of the display, indicating greater importance than those placed toward the center. This is because the food is arranged on a turntable, a kind of lazy Susan, and as the diner turns the disk, the outside dishes are the most accessible. Onion dishes, as side dishes, are always set on the inside, at the center of the display.

In the Beijing area, onions had a particular standing because in the local dialect of Mandarin, the spoken word for onion and the word for clever, though completely different written characters, sound very similar. An onion is placed in a baby's first bath and a line is drawn down the baby's body. Then a man who is considered clever, and ideally tall, throws the onion into the street. The baby can then grow up to be tall and clever.

Traditionally, Japanese use the Welsh onion, known in Tokyo as *naganegi*, which means "long onion"; Welsh onions can extend to a length of 16 inches, sometimes with a diameter of up to one inch. They are also called *shironegi*, which means "white onion," because they remain white about halfway up from the roots. Sometimes they are called *Tokyo negi*, Tokyo onions, because they are central to Tokyo cooking.

In Osaka, which has its own distinct cuisine, *aonegi*, green onions, are used. These are not the same as American green onions, but are closely related to the Tokyo negi except shorter and more green, with very little white. These Japanese onions are light in flavor with a slight bitterness and are far less aggressive than cepa bulbs, and this makes them better suited to the subtle style of Japanese cooking.

In Osaka, aonegi is frequently used to make *sarashi-negi*, a kind of condiment. The onions are finely chopped and wrapped in cheesecloth and then gently rinsed to wash off the juicy slime on the leaves. The chopped onions are sprinkled on food like an herb.

.   .   .

The Sumerians, who lived in the fertile crescent between the Tigris and Euphrates Rivers, in what is present-day Iraq, are often credited for the first written record of eating onions, but they are often credited for the first written record of many things, because they were the first to develop a written language, slightly more than 5,000 years ago, around 3300 B.C.E. The Sumerians left behind clay tablets with their alphabet, cuneiform—written with a triangular stylus imprinting geometric configurations in the clay—which modern linguists have learned how to read. Among the first records on these tablets are the first written recipes for alliums.

Their land, Mesopotamia, Greek for "the land between the rivers," was famous for its fertile soil and gave rise to the myth of the Garden of Eden. In this garden-like environment, with considerable agricultural skill, a range of wild plants were culti-vated for food, including perhaps dozens of different types of onions and also garlic, shallots, chives, and leeks. Traces of onions have been found in the remains of the great royal gardens from four thousand years ago. Onions were not savored only by royalty, though. Among the 282 laws written in the 1792 B.C.E. Code of Hammurabi, stored in the Babylonian temple, was a policy of providing all poor people with a monthly ration of bread and onions.

Four tablets of recipes have been found. Three of them date to before 1730 B.C.E. and one as much as a thousand years later. Although some of the recipes include cooking instructions, they assume knowledge of the cooking techniques of the day, leaving a modern interpreter to sometimes guess at how these dishes were prepared. One tablet contains twenty-five recipes in seventy-five lines. At the bottom it states, "Twenty-one meat stews. Four green."

Many of the recipes involve onions, garlic, and leeks in the same dish. Persian shallots, *Allium stipitatum*, were also used. Today these are rarely cultivated, but they are still harvested wild and sold in Iran. Some of the recipes call for something called *samidu*. This is generally believed to be some type of allium, although it has also been suggested that it was soapwort, a perennial herb usually used, as the name implies, in the making of soap. Scholars experimented with using soapwort in the recipe and found it unbearably bitter and returned to the idea that samidu is a type of forgotten allium. For stews, alliums were often used twice: at the beginning for the savory flavor, and at the end for a sharp edge. This technique is sometimes still used today in Iraqi cooking, though more often with garlic.

A simple recipe on one of the tablets, for *puhadi*, which is translated as lamb stew, calls for lamb with tail fat and salt, dried barley cakes, onion, Persian shallots, and milk, to which crushed leeks and garlic are added. Another stew, called *tah'u*, is made by browning lamb and onions in sheep tail fat, adding coriander, kurrat (leek), cumin, and other spices, and cooking it in beer.

Attempts by culinary historians to make these recipes have resulted in dishes similar to those of contemporary Iraq, which makes Iraq's the oldest recorded cuisine.

.   .   .

It is not certain when onions became ubiquitous, or whether Middle Eastern onions and seeds were traded or widely cultivated. In the Bronze Age, beginning about 3000 B.C.E., trade was extensive. The Bronze Age was a time when the stone tools of the Stone Age were replaced by tools of bronze, and, not surprisingly, the first records of bronze being made were from the Sumerians, who smelted copper with tin. By 2500 B.C.E., trade routes from the Middle East extended to Egypt and across the northern Mediterranean to Turkey to France to Italy, through Germany to Denmark, and from Denmark to Scotland and England. Eastward trade moved through Asia Minor all the way to Beijing and down the western coast of India to Sumatra, Java, and New Guinea. Onions and onion seeds probably traveled some of these routes.

Onions were clearly a staple food in ancient Egypt. According to Herodotus, dubbed the "father of history" for his meticulous methodology, workers on the pyramids in about 2575 B.C.E., whoever they were, were fed onions for strength. The Hebrew Bible states that Hebrew slaves built the pyramids, though Egyptians have no record of this. Even if not, onions seem to have been part of the Hebrew diet. In the Book of Numbers, it is written that the hungry Hebrews, having left Egypt and now free in the desert, were stuck with no onions and nothing but manna from heaven. This was apparently an unenviable situation. They complained to Moses, "We remember the fish we ate in Egypt that cost nothing, the cucumbers, the melons, the leeks, the onions, and the garlic. There is nothing at all beside the manna before our eyes." Apparently they were bored with this perfect gift from heaven, this mysterious food from God, manna, and just wanted some onions. They missed the whole onion family. Moses was not pleased. If you free your people and give them food from God, you don't expect them to complain, "But where's the onions?"

Onions were eaten throughout the ancient Mediterranean world. Hippocrates said Cyprus onions were the strongest and those of Cnidos the mildest. The smallest were from Tuscany and the whitest from Sardis. Pliny the Elder listed many onions of interest, including shallots, along with their medicinal and gastronomic properties. He wrote that round onions were more succulent than flat ones, a theory that would not be accepted today, since many of the most praised onions today are flat. But he also claimed that the most flavorful onions were red, a point on which he would get some agreement today.

Pliny did not regard Roman onions as among the better ones and wrote that the onions called "Gallic onions, a smaller species, were more delicate and preferable to those grown on the Roman peninsula." But he did admire the onions of Pompeii, although in that city onions seemed to have a low standing and onion growers were not allowed in the guild of vegetable growers. In the lava fields that are now all that is left of the Roman city buried by the eruption of Mount Vesuvius in 79 C.E., remains of onion fields have been identified, fossilized in lava like the dwellers of the city. Pliny took a boat and tried to rescue friends from Pompeii and died in the effort.

Romans found onions, which preserve well, to be an excellent provision for soldiers to carry in their travels of conquest throughout Europe. Perhaps they did not realize how readily available they were, or perhaps in some parts of Europe there were no onions to be had.

Though there is ample evidence that Romans were onion eaters, food historians often comment that Apicius's book from first-century-C.E. Rome, often cited as the first known cookbook, did not give onion recipes. Apicius, however, is not a good role model for gourmets. He spent his entire inheritance on rare and expensive food items, and then when the money was gone, imposing an end to his gourmetism, he killed himself. Actually he did this some time before the book appeared, which has led some to wonder who wrote this book that has no onion recipes. But while there are no onion recipes, there are a number of recipes for bulbs, *bulbos*, and onions were probably one of several that could have been used in these dishes. Or did he prefer more exotic bulbs?

Apicius said that bulbs should be served with olive oil, broth, and vinegar, with a light dusting of cumin. He also gave recipes for frying, for a bulb puree, and for bulbs seasoned with thyme, oregano, honey, and vinegar, reduced with wine, date wine, broth, and a splash of olive oil. In Pliny's time, onions, like most vegetables, were used in making appetizers. Apicius recommended as an appetizer seasoning bulbs in garum, a popular fermented fish sauce, and olive oil and wine and then cooking them with pork liver and chicken and thickening the sauce with a starch.

.   .   .

In his 1419 recipe collection, Chiquart, the royal cook for the Duke of Savoy, shows a strong preference for accompanying meats with cooked onions. The onions were always chopped very fine and browned in lard before being poured over the main dish.

If the legend is to be believed, Hungary was one of the last countries to embrace onions. Beatrice, or Beatrix, of Naples, the Italian wife of Matthias, the Austrian-born Hapsburg king of Hungary and Croatia from 1458 to 1490, introduced many things to Hungary. Some of this may be apocryphal, but Beatrice certainly was memorable. She tried to succeed her husband to the throne against his wishes and staged an illegal marriage to a successor, which was thrown out by the pope. Along the way she is said to have introduced chess playing, figs, marzipan, and onions to Hungary. All of these have certainly been central to Hungarian culture ever since, although it is difficult to believe that Hungarians had no onions, by then common throughout Europe, until the fifteenth century. It is known that she valued getting onions shipped to her, either because there weren't any in Hungary or they weren't of the same quality. A letter survives from her to her sister, Eleanora, in which she says, "Thanks for the onions and garlic sent me from Ferrara. The king could not have been more pleased if they had been pearls." In any event it was in the fifteenth century that Hungary developed a rich and elaborate cuisine, and onions were at the center of most of the savory dishes.

The English may have been even slower to onionize. Giacomo Castelvetro, who was rescued from the Inquisition in his native Italy in 1613 by the British, was appalled by the way the English ate—especially by the lack of vegetables and salad. He encouraged the British to eat more onions, and recommended them with crushed black pepper.

·   ·   ·

As with mathematics, literature, astronomy, and many other subjects, the Arabs were far ahead of Europeans on onions. In the sophisticated cooking of medieval North Africa, onion flavor was often derived not from the use of chopped onions, but by squeezing the bulbs and seasoning only with onion juice. This idea was also used in the West; in fact Fannie Farmer, in the 1896 edition of her cookbook, explains how to rub onions on a grater

Loading bags of onions, Rice County, Minnesota, 1939.

and make onion juice. But she did not use the juice in any of her recipes. In America, onion juice was mixed with sugar and coffee as a cold remedy, and this is what she recommended. But in Arab cooking, it was an ingredient.

Starting a stew by sautéing meat with onions, as the Sumerians had done, was commonplace in medieval Arab cooking. In Andalusia, the part of southern Spain that was Arab-ruled the longest, there is a nicely rhythmic saying, "*Olla sin cebolla, es baile sin tamborín*"—"a stew without onions is like a dance without a tambourine."

O. Henry, the fabled nineteenth-century American writer, wrote an entire short story, "The Third Ingredient," about the dilemma of making a stew with no onions available. He said that a stew without onions lacked soul. "There's certain things in life that are naturally intended to fit and belong together. One is beef and potatoes with onions." The story states that "a stew without an onion is worse'n a matinee without candy," which was exactly the Andalusian point about the tambourines.

From very early times, onions were valued not only as food, but also for their skins, which were found to be a useful dye. Perhaps the earliest use of onion-skin dye was to darken stews and broths. In many countries, including France at the time of the Renaissance, onions were baked for several days at low temperatures in a bread oven until they became fairly dark and were sold in the market to be placed in a stock to make the broth darker. Onion skins remain one of the most popular natural dyes. They easily release their tint after simmering a brief time, able to dye wool pink, orange, dark brown, or pastels depending on the quantity and type of skins and accompanying elements. Red onion skins mixed with white skins and indigo can produce a variety of green shades.

Dying eggs for Easter, a European tradition that goes back to at least the thirteenth century, was often done with onion skins. Elena Molokhovets's *A Gift to Young Housewives* was the bible for Russian women in its many editions from the 1860s until the 1917 revolution, when it was deemed too bourgeois. In it, she recommends using onion skins to dye Easter eggs yellow and also to darken broth by boiling onion skins in bouillon.

. . .

The reason that Welsh onions, not from Wales, are confusing is that there is also an onion, the leek, that is important to Welsh history and culture. The Welsh attachment to leeks may date back as far as the fourth century B.C.E. to the ancient Druids, priests in Celtic culture, who were great nature worshippers. The

Druids are thought to have originated the Welsh belief that leek broth cures the sick and lessens the pains of childbirth, and that a leek placed under a pillow will let a young maid see her future husband in her sleep.

According to legend, David, the sixth-century patron saint of Wales, had his army wear leeks into battle against the pagan Saxon invaders from England, so that the Welshmen could be recognized. The great battle supposedly occurred in a field of wild leeks or ramsoms. The leekless Saxons were stopped. In the fourteenth century, the renowned Welsh archers dressed in green and white, the colors of a leek. In Shakespeare's *Henry V*, King Henry declares his Welshness by wearing a leek into battle. Welsh fans still wear leeks to Welsh rugby matches and it is still traditional to wear a leek on March 1, St. David's Day.

In the Middle Ages there were many recipes in Wales for onions and few for leeks, but later the proportion was reversed. It is thought that the later leek recipes were mostly older onion recipes that had substituted leeks. But the onion recipes remain. One seventeenth-century Welsh onion recipe calls for butter and beef stock. *Tiesen nionod*, onion cake, alternates layers of onions and potatoes.

Leeks grow extremely well in Welsh soil. They are sturdy, survive harsh winters, and have been an inexpensive, easily available food not only in Wales, but in northern France and England too. Chaucer's expression for something that was worthless was "not worth a leek."

But leeks are becoming less Welsh. Welsh football fans have started wearing daffodils rather than leeks, because the Welsh name for the flower is *cenhinen Bedr*, or Peter's leek. The first flowers of spring, they bloom just in time for St. David's Day. It may also be that people would rather wear a flower than an onion.

· · ·

In many parts of Europe, old-time onion traditions are celebrated at folk festivals. One of the most cherished local onions are the calçots, grown in the Catalan region of Spain. The calçots are green onions, as large as leeks, but stronger-tasting, though milder than Spanish onions. In the nineteenth century, Catalan farmers started growing them with the bottoms covered in soil so that they remained white up to their green tips, a technique also used in Belgium for endive and for white asparagus. The name *calçot* means "stocking," because the green onions appear to wear a white stocking.

Throughout Catalonia are held traditional winter onion festivals, free-spirited Lenten bashes known as *calçotadas*. The most famous is in Valls the last week of January. Calçots were originally a winter crop, but by popular demand the season has been extended into spring.

At calçotadas, these onions are charcoal grilled, traditionally on grapevine branches saved after the wine harvest, and served hot on a terra-cotta roofing tile. The blackened skin is torn off, the onion is dipped in a special sauce, and then it is popped into the mouth with one's head leaning back to receive it. The sauce is made from almonds, garlic, hazelnuts, olive oil, tomatoes, sweet and hot red peppers, and parsley, and if you are doing this properly, you get the sauce dripped all over you. The onions are usually accompanied by grilled meat or sausages cooked in the charcoal. Eating contests are held at some of the festivals, and champions have been known to consume two hundred or more of these grilled onions in sauce in one sitting.

There are places where being a champion onion eater counts.

3

The Americas Know
Their Onions

O nions remained predominantly a wild plant in the Americas much longer than in Europe and Asia.

The French explorer Jacques Marquette, traveling the shore of what is now Lake Michigan in 1674, relied for nourishment on an onion that the Indigenous locals called *cigaga-wunj*, which means "onion place" and is the origin of the name *Chicago*. In more recent times it has come to be known as the Canada onion, *Allium canadense*, and it grows wild in much of North America from New Brunswick to Florida and west to the Rocky Mountains. It is fairly easy to spot because it has a very strong onion scent and it flowers spectacularly in great globes of little pink or white blossoms. Today it is favored as an ornamental plant.

But some historians and naturalists insist that the wild onion that gave Chicago its name was actually the nodding wild onion, *Allium cernuum*. It is called nodding because it does not stand erect and, unusual for onions, is bent over even when flowering. It announces itself with white or deep pink or rose flowers with a strong scent of onion. According to a description from the 1890s, these onions look "bright on the whole since the reddish hues prevail. They are often in such quantities and grow so thickly that little else is noticeable where they stand."

Such bright wild patches are a very rare sight today, even in their native habitat such as the Chicago area, though they are also found in Michigan, Minnesota, Iowa, Wisconsin, Illinois, Saskatchewan, and Ontario.

.   .   .

There are seventy species of wild onion native to North America. Native American Indians harvested them and sometimes ate them raw, but also used them to flavor cooked dishes or would eat them as a cooked vegetable. Onions were also used in syrups and in dyeing. Roasted wild onions and honey were used by Native Americans to treat snakebites.

There does not appear to have been much cultivation of alliums by Native North Americans, with the notable exception of the Aztecs. But Europeans could not imagine life without cultivated onions and so brought them with them.

Christopher Columbus, apparently finding no onions on his first voyage to the Caribbean, which was a voyage of exploration, brought along onion seeds, cattle, horses, and sheep on his second voyage, which was a voyage of colonization. In 1494 his crew planted onions in what is now the Dominican Republic.

But Mexicans may have already cultivated alliums. Hernán Cortés, in his march of conquest from Vera Cruz to Tenochtitlán, now Mexico City, found that the local people cooked onions, leeks, and garlic. According to Cortés, they ate an onion called *xonacatl*. This is a word in Nahuatl, the original Aztec language that is still in use. Today it means "onion," but what kind of onion the original xonacatl was is not certain. In Mayan the word is *kukut*. Francisco Hernández, a physician to Philip II of Spain, was sent to Mexico from 1570 to 1577 to report on the flora. According to Hernández, xonacatl was an onion with a "split roof," which probably meant a split bulb, more like a shallot.

Pre-Spanish cooking, much of which is still in practice, does not use a great deal of alliums. The rich sauces called *moles* involved dozens of ground-up ingredients but rarely an onion. The famous mole from Puebla, *mole poblana*, uses some five different chili peppers, chocolate, ground tortilla, seeds, and a dozen other ingredients including garlic, but no onions. *Mole manchamanteles* does include both boiled onions and garlic on its long ingredient list. *Mole de olla* also uses both onions and garlic.

It is far easier to trace pre-Spanish Mexican cooking than Sumerian, because the Spanish recorded what they found and the Indigenous people still have their culture and are continuing to cook the dishes they made before the Spanish arrived. Some modern inventions have crept in. City tortillas now are made by machine, but the people in Indigenous villages think this is a disgrace and tortillas there are still made by hand, exclusively by women. Recipes still call for xonacatl, but today cooks usually use the onion the Spanish brought. This is historian Heriberto García Rivas's recipe for xonacatl in his cookbook *Cocina prehispánica mexicana*:

> In a little hot chia oil, fry three onions finely chopped. Add three ripe zucchini squash, peeled and quartered, a tablespoon of yucca or sweet potato flour, stir with a wooden spoon, mix in six large peeled and seeded tomatoes, maguey or corn syrup, salt, pepper, herbs, cook slowly.

. . .

It is not certain that the Indigenous people of the Pacific Northwest ate the bulbs of wild onions, but it is known that, like ancient Europeans, they ate other bulbs. They were particularly fond of camas, *Camassia quamash*, which, like onions, used to be thought of as a lily variety. More recent botanists have decided it is in the family of the agave.

White pioneers learned to eat camas in desperate times, noting that it was similar to but sweeter than an onion. But there is another camas that is deadly poisonous, known as "the death camas," which grows among the edible camas and creates understandable reluctance among newcomers to harvest these bulbs. After the Nez Perce gave some good camas to Lewis and Clark, Lewis described it as "a tunicated bulb, much the consistence, shape and appearance of the onion; glutinous or somewhat slymy when chewed." He thought lilies and hyacinths tasted better.

As in Europe, Native Americans were extremely fond of the wild onion called ramps, or ramson, a strong-smelling species. They cooked ramps as a vegetable sautéed in acorn oil. These alliums are among the first green vegetables to come up in the spring when little else is available and so were greatly valued, even used in religious rites by some tribes, including Chippewa, Cherokee, Ojibwa, Menominee, and Iroquois.

Early European colonists considered eating ramps to be a desperate move, and their smell was associated with extreme poverty, but they learned from Native Americans and these wild vegetables became an important resource for starving settlers. Native Americans continue to value these wild plants, but because of overharvesting and destruction of wild lands, they are becoming hard to find. They often grow undisturbed on the lands of national parks, but the reason they are undisturbed is that picking wild plants from national parks is illegal.

Native groups have tried to be granted an exception, but that is a difficult fight. Cherokee were charged in 2009 with illegally harvesting ramps from the Great Smoky Mountains National Park, despite the park being situated on their traditional plant-gathering lands. This is an ongoing fight for a number of Native American groups.

Europeans preferred cultivated onions because that was what they were used to. One hundred and fifty years after Columbus, there were still few onions cultivated in the Caribbean or North America. When Richard Ligon, escaping the English Civil War, moved to Barbados in 1647, he carried with him not only seeds for sage, tarragon, parsley, and marjoram, but also onion seeds, and thus began Barbados's onion cultivation.

The first Pilgrims brought onions with them on the *Mayflower*. Onions were planted in Massachusetts in 1629 and in Virginia in 1648. The founding father known to be a great onion eater, George Washington, seemed passionate about them, and ordered onions to be planted at Mount Vernon, according to a 1798 report. Thomas Jefferson left detailed accounts that show that onions were a staple crop on his Virginia estate, Monticello, before, during, and after the Revolutionary War, and even on land he owned before construction began on the estate in 1769. He seemed to have favored white Spanish onions, but Madeira and tree onions were also planted.

Amelia Simmons, author of the first cookbook published in independent America, in Hartford in 1796, recommended Madeira white onions if you prefer a "softer" flavor and "not too fiery." But, like Pliny, she also recommended red onions.

By 1806 the new Americans were raising six varieties of onions, and by the time of the Civil War, there were fourteen popular varieties.

.   .   .

The Easterners who went west in the mid-nineteenth century found few onions under cultivation. They greatly missed them, even though they liked to call them "skunk eggs" because of their strong smell. Because of their ability to store well, onions later became a basic provision for migrating pioneers on the wagons that went west. An 1860 issue of *Hutchings' California Magazine* listed onions as one of the "necessities" for an eight-day journey into the mountains.

Elizabeth Bacon Custer, the widow of the infamous George Armstrong Custer, did not write of his racism and genocide, but she did write about onions while camping in the west with Custer, saying that they were "as rare out there, and more appreciated than pomegranates are in New York."

Custer and his younger brother Tom, who also died on the Little Bighorn, were zealous cepaphiles. But apparently, in a rare criticism, Elizabeth was not fond of her husband's onion breath. In an 1873 letter to his wife while on an expedition to the Yellowstone River, Custer wrote that he was filling up on onions now that he was away from her. "I supped on RAW ONIONS; I will probably breakfast, lunch and dine on them tomorrow, and the next day, and the day after ad libitum ad infinitum . . . Go it old fellow! Make the most of your liberties! . . . If you intend to eat raw onions now is your only time for 'missus is comin.'"

Custer seems to have taken onions as he found them, but some Americans wanted more—they wanted them bigger, smaller, stronger, milder, sweeter. In the twentieth and twenty-first centuries onions were to become big business.

4

Looking for the Perfect Onion

Onions are the second most produced vegetable in the world, beaten only by tomatoes. Considering what an odd plant it is, this is a surprising victory over such tame contestants as cucumbers and lettuce. Even garlic only comes in as number ten. True, onions run a distant second—177 metric tons of tomatoes are produced every year and only 93.17 metric tons of onions. But they are not competitors, often being planted together to help each other.

Of the 9.2 million acres of onions harvested in the world each year, only 8 percent is traded internationally. Most onions everywhere are grown for the home market. China by far produces the most onions in the world and India is second. This is not surprising since these are the two most populous countries. As an onion producer the United States is a distant third. Egypt, the fourth largest, is significantly behind the United States but produces great quantities of onions on the banks of the Nile for a population, as in ancient times, of still dedicated onion eaters.

American onion farmers are efficient. They produce 6.75 billion pounds of onions annually on about 125,000 acres of land. Fewer than one thousand onion farmers accomplish all this, contributing less than 1 percent to the U.S. economy.

But the public demand for onions in America has been steadily increasing for decades. In 1970 Americans ate an average of 10.14 pounds per year. By 2018 the average had risen to 20.39 pounds, doubling consumption in less than fifty years. Far more onions are now consumed per capita in the United States than in most countries. World onion consumption averages less than 14 pounds per person, so Americans qualify as major onion eaters.

India is famous for the flavorfulness of its onions. It exports to numerous countries, but especially to Nepal, Bangladesh, Malaysia, Sri Lanka, and the United Arab Emirates. There are usually two good harvests, one from November to January, and a second from January to May. The success of these harvests is important to the well-being of the states of Maharashtra, Karnataka, Gujarat, and Madhya Pradesh.

This is a fat swath of the middle of the Indian subcontinent, distanced from the power center of New Delhi but with the major port of Mumbai on the Arabian Sea in Maharashtra. More than a third of India's onions are grown in Maharashtra alone. The role

Women sort, grade, and sell onions at the agriculture producer market, a wholesale market in Nagpur, Maharashtra State, in the heart of agricultural India. Photo by S. Sudarshan, 2022.

onions play in the economy is something no Indian government can afford to forget. When onion prices rise, angry people march in the streets of Maharashtra, sometimes wearing garlands of onions. But also those who consume the most onions are the more politically powerful people of northern India.

Indians are onion eaters. In an elaborate and regionally varied cuisine, onions are part of almost every savory dish. The ultimate dish on which the poor survive in Maharashtra, *kanda bhakri*, is a flatbread eaten with raw onions. A shortage of onions, as happened in 1998, 2010, 2015, and 2019, is a crisis. Onion prices were believed to have brought down the national government in the 1980 election. Indira Gandhi triumphed with a national campaign that used the high prices of onions as a symbol of economic mismanagement.

It was widely believed that the high price of onions was the principal cause of the defeat of the Bharatiya Janata Party in the 1998 Delhi Assembly elections. In 2013 onions became so expensive that a plot to steal a truck loaded with onions was launched, but the robbers were caught.

In 2019, drought followed by heavy monsoon rains resulted in a shortage of onions, causing the price to rise. This put the government of Prime Minister Narendra Modi in crisis mode, even though he had just won an unexpected landslide for a second five-year term. Onions were a leading headline in Indian newspapers. His Hindu nationalist policies, hostility to Pakistan, and abuse of Indian Muslims have been harshly criticized in India's intellectual class and internationally, but his greatest vulnerability in India has been the dissatisfaction of farmers. The onion crisis has fueled that anger. Ironically, Modi started encouraging onion imports, even from Pakistan, a Muslim country he usually denigrates.

Modi prohibited what he called the hording of onions, storing them for later. Normally onions from the spring harvest, especially in Maharashtra, have a low moisture content, which makes them suitable for storage. Farmers keep them dry on raised platforms known as *kanda chawls*. These stored onions were destined for export, but in 2019 Modi banned them from leaving the country. Without Indian imports, the price of onions in Bangladesh leapt 700 percent. Many vendors there stopped selling onions at all, because the public was so angry about their prices. In Nepal, also dependent on Indian imports, onions were vanishing from markets as well.

Banning exports caused onion prices in India to lower somewhat, but it also meant that the Indian economy was being deprived of one of its major exports. And with the onion supply still low, the onion producers in Maharashtra were angry that they were losing their high prices.

. . .

Onions have always been an imported product in Britain. Though onions grew wild, the people there were never regular onion eaters until the Romans started to bring them. When the Normans conquered England in 1066, they carried onions with them as well. In 1699 John Evelyn wrote that the best onions were brought in from Spain.

Onions were eaten by all, but they were a food the poor could depend on. The seventeenth-century Scottish gardening expert John Reid suggested, "Onions may be baked in a little butter if you want [lack] meat." In Dickens's day, a slice of onion on a slice of bread was standard working-class fare in England.

The British always had the idea that their farming land was too scarce and precious to use for onions. But they planted onions wherever else they went, from North America to the Caribbean to Australia. When the first British settlers went to Australia in 1787, they took seeds with them and it is thought that this was when onions were introduced to the continent. A long-standing assumption that the aboriginal societies, before Europeans, cultivated no crops has been called into question. But it is not known if they cultivated onions or harvested wild ones. There is the legend of the "bush onion," which they did gather and eat, but this plant is not a true onion and in fact is not even related to an allium.

· · ·

Roscoff is a port town on the north coast of the far tip of the Finistère, the seaward end of the Brittany peninsula. It is the heart of Brittany, a Celtic region with its own Celtic language and a culture that has struggled to survive French control. While most of the seaports in the area are known for their seafood, Roscoff is known for its onions. According to Alexandre Dumas père, in the nineteenth century this area of Brittany had more onions than any other part of France.

Roscoff grows a unique variety of *Allium cepa* known as *oignon rosé de Roscoff*, the Roscoff pink onion. The sandy soil of the Finistère is one of the few places where this variety prospers. They have reddish-pink skin, white flesh, and a strong flavor. Not a native variety, they seemed to have come in from the port trade in the seventeenth century and then flourished as a local crop. With continual breeding in the area, they have become particularly well adapted to this climate and soil and have a high yield per acre. There are other onions in the region: the Erdeven, which are yellowish pink with white flesh and little skin, and the yellow onions by the bay of Yffiniac.

The pink Roscoffs became famous in Britain. Bretons had been selling their onions to the British since the fourteenth century and possibly earlier. Trade across the Channel was stopped by the Napoleonic Wars, but in 1815, when the narrow waterway that separated France from England was once again opened for trade, northern French ports eagerly looked for products to sell.

Roscoff's onions were taken to Plymouth by sturdy young men who festooned their bicycles with quantities of onions tied in long ropes, making their bikes look like bulky two-wheeled yaks. They usually arrived in July and stayed until Christmas, often finding places to store their onions by the docks. Some sailed over in November and returned home in February or March when it was time to help with planting.

Johnnies on the road, selling onions in Britain.

They pedaled all over southern England and far up into Scotland selling their onions and, it's unclear why, became known as "Johnnies." Periodically they would have to return to a base in the south to restock. Often they shouted as they pedaled through the streets, "Buy my good onions!" According to Dumas's *Grand dictionnaire de cuisine*, they would pick fights, saying, "The English onion is not good." But it should be kept in mind that Dumas, of *Count of Monte Cristo* and *Three Musketeers* fame, was predominantly a fiction writer.

The Johnnies had a hard life, often finding only shops to sleep in. But they had more standing than the poor Irish women who sold local onions. For many years British people who had never been to France had in their minds a stereotype of a Frenchman as one who wore a striped Breton shirt and a beret and rode a bicycle. Those were Johnnies.

More than a thousand Johnnies traveled to England each year. For almost two centuries, Johnnies were a common sight in England and a standard source for buying much-appreciated pink onions. Then the trade started to die out, replaced by more efficient importers, and a Johnnie in the 1990s was said to be the last one.

In Britain onions are still largely imported (but are no longer carried about by bicycle), though there are a few British who do grow onions. One of those famous British eccentricities is the urge to grow the largest onion. Farmers compete. A Scottish farmer named Rodgers established a 1980 record with a 6.5-pound onion, despite John Evelyn writing in 1699 of an 8-pound onion. Several 7-pounders claimed records in the 1980s, and soon after records were broken at the Harrogate Autumn Flower Show in

North Yorkshire when Tony Glover came in with a monster onion weighing 18 pounds 11.84 ounces, which he triumphantly hoisted above his lean body. Guinness World Records claims the record, also from the Harrogate show in 2012, is Peter Glazebrook's 18-pound 1-ounce onion, though this would be slightly lighter than Glover's.

Competitive British onion growers concentrate on certain varieties that are known for size, such as Oakey, Ailsa Craig, and Kelsae—not household names except among those who really know their (big) onions. The Oakey was developed in the 1870s from a white Spanish onion and became celebrated in the Midlands for its 2-pound bulbs, for winning contests, and for storing well. The Ailsa Craig was also developed in the nineteenth century, from a Portuguese seed at a Scottish castle, and was named after a rock at sea that was visible from the castle.

But so few onions in England were homegrown that in 1939 when World War II closed off trade with the continent, Britain found itself onionless. The government urged the public to start growing more onions, but to no avail. Onions became a rare and expensive luxury food. Even today, more than half the onions consumed in Britain are imported.

.   .   .

One way in which the British tried to ensure their onion supply was via the colonies. In 1616, Governor Daniel Tucker, a farmer by trade, took onion seeds to Bermuda on board a British ship, the *Edwin*. The island proved ideal for growing sweet, unusually mild onions and soon they were being exported back to England. By 1830 onions were a major Bermuda crop and an important export. Though only a 21-square-mile island, Bermuda had 50 acres devoted to cultivating onions. Along with the first onion seeds, the first enslaved person from Africa was taken to Bermuda from the Caribbean on board the *Edwin*. Enslaved children would run through the fields chasing away the birds that ate the onion seeds. This was called "minding the onion seed." The work passed on to free Black immigrants after Emancipation in 1834.

In 1849 a ship from Bermuda, *The Golden Rule*, picked up the first of many Portuguese immigrants in Madeira. Madeira's culture was centered on the cultivation, eating, and trading of onions. They grew enormous quantities. Madeira onions were soon to become a staple in the Caribbean and much of Latin America.

The Portuguese greatly expanded onion cultivation and other Bermuda agriculture. New Yorkers called Bermuda "the Onion Patch" and called the merchant marines who sold the onions to the rest of the world "Onions." Bermuda onions were shipped in baskets woven of palmetto leaves, the same native leaves used to swat away birds from the fields.

Later in the nineteenth century, Mark Twain became a regular visitor to Bermuda, and in 1878 he wrote *Rambling Notes of an Idle Excursion* about his trip there the previous year. He noted, "The onion is the pride and joy of Bermuda. It is her jewel, her gem of gems. In her conversation, her pulpit, her literature, it is her most frequent and eloquent figure. In Bermuda metaphor it stands for perfection—perfection absolute."

The unforeseen beginning of the end was in 1898, when Bermuda seeds were planted in South Texas near Cotulla. These sweet yellow onions proved popular, and so more were planted. By 1909 Bermuda onions grew in twelve Texas counties. Onion exports from Bermuda were stopped due to World War I, but by 1918, when Bermuda could once again export, Texas production had become huge. The United States then imposed high tariffs to stop competition from Bermuda, and Bermuda onions became firmly established as a Texas product with which the small island could not compete. Today only a few small-scale farms on Bermuda produce onions. Most of the onions on Bermuda are now imported.

The transplanting and tariff protection of Bermuda onions in Texas was the origin of what is now the state's largest agricultural sector, though Texas still produces fewer onions than California and Washington.

.   .   .

With the exception of a few specialties such as cipollinis, small flat onions from the Emilia-Romagna region of Italy, or local varieties from certain regions, most consumers in the world know little about what onion they are eating. They choose large or small; yellow, white, or red.

But there is a tremendous variety of onions. Recipes can be deceptive, because some onions are stronger than others. Climate and soil—especially sulfur content and drainage—and, according to some, even phases of the moon, can have a tremendous impact on the nature of an onion.

For centuries, bees and other pollinating insects randomly crossed onions. But this was not a regular event. The onion produces what is known as a "perfect flower," a flower with closely knit male and female parts that can pollinate itself and doesn't need bees to reproduce. This produced only a few inconsistent variations. Even when nature produced a crossbreed, it was not striving for a trait that would be of interest to humans.

However, today 90 to 95 percent of onions produced in the United States are artificially mixed strains. Such hybrids originally had very low yields. But this began to change with the work of an Arizona geneticist, Henry A. Jones.

To create hybrids, a flower that was only female and thus was receptive to outside male input was necessary. Otherwise the flower favored its own organisms. Scientists worked at "emasculating onions"—removing the male parts. Since male and female parts were very close together, emasculation was a tedious and demanding effort performed with tweezers. The breakthrough came in 1925 when an Italian red onion was found in the University of California Davis plot that had only female parts and therefore could not pollinate itself. According to Jones, "the history of practically all hybrid onion seeds produced in the United States today can be traced back to [this] single male-sterile (female) onion plant . . . in 1925."

Once able to create hybrids, Jones found that at least some of their offspring had female-only flowers, which enabled him to continue crossbreeding. From 1925 to 1943, using flies for pollination, Jones developed crossbred onions with a higher yield per acre, uniform plants and bulbs, and greater resistance to disease. Some of his onions were three times the weight of the original bulbs from which they were bred. He headed research at the Desert Seed Company in El Centro, California, which became one of the leading sources of onion seeds for American farmers.

Once hybrid seeds became easily available, commercial farmers never again relied on the vagaries of their own seeds, but were able to buy exactly what they wanted.

Onion seeds are small, black, and triangular; they look like little shards of coal. Usually these little black seeds are planted in seedbeds and a farmer knows that the seedlings are doing well when they produce roots at least as long as the green shoots produced on top. Once they have substantial roots and shoots, they are planted in the field, usually about one foot apart. Any closer would inhibit the growth of the bulb.

. . .

In the 1930s, experiments in breeding onions began in Texas with cooperation from Jones. The "Grano 502" variety was developed. The original Grano came from the town of Grano near Toledo, Spain. The Texas Grano 502 is the parent of a growing American market, the "sweet onion." These are onions that are less pungent, less stinging to the eyes, and contain more sugar, so that they are literally sweeter tasting. From these come the Texas supersweet and the Granex, similar to the Grano, but with a flatter shape.

In 1932, Moses Coleman, a farmer in Tombs County in south-eastern Georgia, was looking for a good cash crop and decided to try onions. He bought Bermuda onion seeds from Texas. This was before Grano and Granex were developed. He harvested a crop in the late spring and was surprised to find that they lacked the characteristic aggressive bite of other raw onions. They were sweet-tasting and barely caused a tear when he cut into one.

At first people didn't want to buy them because they were not what an onion is supposed to be. But he found his market, and even sold them for a higher price than normal onions. This was at the height of the Depression and other struggling farmers noticed Coleman's success and started growing these sweet onions too. The sandy soil with a low sulfur content, just the right amount of rainfall most years, and warm temperatures produced mild onions. In the heart of this region was the town of Vidalia, where major routes intersected. In the 1940s a farmers' market was built there by the State of Georgia. The sweet onions were the most popular product of the market and they became known as Vidalia onions.

In 1952 Texas Granex seeds were brought in and they became the standard Vidalia seed. As production increased, the State of Georgia took an interest in branding the product. To be called Vidalia onions they had to be grown either within thirteen counties or parts of seven others—a distinct geographic area, about 10,000 acres in all, stretching from west of coastal Savannah to McRae in the center of the southern end of the state. Ideally, each field is rotated with another crop every other year, usually soybeans or peanuts.

A typical Vidalia onion farm is 300 to 400 acres but there are a few that are over a thousand. A few family farms have only 50 acres. But these sweet Granex hybrid onions are not suited for large-scale production because the higher the sugar content, the more fragile the plant, so these high-sugar onions require careful handling. There are about twenty-five varieties, but they are all flat shaped. Some would prefer a rounded onion like a Grano, better for slicing for such popular dishes as onion rings. But a Vidalia has been defined. It is a sweet, flat onion. Every year the Georgia Agricultural Commission states an official "pack date."

An onion sold before that date does not have the legal right to be called a Vidalia onion.

It is an expensive onion to produce, given that it is planted, harvested, and cured by hand. The seeds themselves are expensive. And they do not get the enormous yields of some of the western onion fields in Washington, California, Arizona, and Texas. A certain amount of pesticides is used depending on the year, to defend against crickets that move in right after planting and the attack of certain deadly pathogens. Irrigation is used to get the right amount of water. Too much water or not enough water will destroy the crop. After harvesting, the onions lie between five and seven days curing in the field unless it rains, and then they must be quickly moved to well-aerated drying pens, another reason why large holdings are more difficult.

Bob Stafford, former director of a research and promotion organization called the Vidalia Onion Committee, said, "It takes a certain kind of person to handle the rough times."

Even so, Vidalias have become a big business, with about 200 million pounds of these hand-grown onions sold around North America annually. Marketing became more elaborate, with an annual onion festival to attract tourists and even a Vidalia Onion Hall of Fame that elected one inductee each year.

People in south Georgia know their onions. While most Americans are just choosing which color, in Vidalia country, customers have favorite farms. Some farmers are more conscientious than others. Conscientious means a better product but often less profit. Stafford said, "Some people pump them up with a lot of fertilizer to grow fast and they won't be as sweet and mild. The only way to test them is to bite in." Some prefer them a little

Stella Gutowski, "Queen Stella," at the Onion Festival of the 1940 World's Fair in New York. Two hundred costumed singers and dancers performed.

stronger and others a little milder. You have to know your farm. Some say they like an onion that won't even sting your eyes, but Stafford said that there will always be a little sting. "An onion is an onion."

· · ·

Sweet onions require a perfect microclimate, the right soil, and, above all, an absence of sulfur, which is the ammunition for an onion attack. They also require a certain breed of artisanal farmer, someone who will settle for a small yield of delicate, carefully handled plants. But the reward is a much higher price than that commanded by other onions.

A number of sweet onions are produced in the United States, including in Florida, California, the Pecos Valley in New Mexico, and the Rio Grande Valley in South Texas. A sweet onion sometimes called the "Million Dollar Baby" is the official state onion of Texas. The Vidalia onion is the official vegetable of the state of Georgia. Fourteen states have official vegetables and in four—Washington and Utah are the other two—that vegetable is the sweet onion.

Vidalias may be the most famous sweet onion, but California's Imperial Valley, which grows a lot of almost everything, grows more sweet onions than Georgia, and Texas produces twice as many as Georgia. There are threatening upstarts in Florida, New York, and other places.

A famous sweet onion is produced in Walla Walla, Washington. According to the official legend, a French soldier, Peter Pieri, found sweet onions growing in Corsica and at the end of the nineteenth century took them to Walla Walla, Washington, which had a community of immigrant farmers, mostly Italian. Situated in the southeastern corner of the state, at the base of the Blue Mountains, Walla Walla had a drier and milder climate than that of the neighboring Cascade Range. What was then called the French onion developed through selective breeding over generations of crops. The mildest Walla Wallas are planted in August and grow over winter.

Another celebrated sweet onion, though not widely distributed, is grown on the Hawaiian island of Maui. The Maui onion began with Chinese indentured laborers taken to Maui to work the sugarcane plantations. Some stayed and started farming an area called Kula. Records show that Chinese immigrants farmed onions in Kula as early as the 1880s. But it was in the 1930s, when they brought in Yellow Bermuda seeds, that Kula first got a reputation for sweet onions.

Kula is a unique microclimate on the slope of Haleakalā, an imposing inactive volcano that dominates the Maui horizon, rising almost 10,000 feet. That is small in the world of volcanoes but looks impressive when viewed from little Maui, three quarters of which is the volcano. It has one of the largest dormant volcano craters in the world, about 20 miles in circumference. Kula is an area halfway up the most gradual side of the volcano, the western slope, a red-soiled arid region as opposed to the other sides, which are lush, green, and rainy. The sulfur level is low on this slope. The Kula elevation is between 1,200 and 4,000 feet. Any higher and the nights would be too cold. Any lower and the days would be too hot and the soil too sulfurous. Onions would still be able to grow but they would not be as mild and sweet as in Kula.

The original Yellow Bermuda onions planted were so sweet and mild that they became known as Kula onions, a special breed. In the 1950s Kula growers started getting better results, as in Vidalia, with a Granex, and the Maui onion became known as a flat-shaped sweet onion.

In the 1970s, Kula onions started being shipped to the mainland United States. But, an expensive onion to begin with, it is much more expensive on the mainland. Hawaii is the most isolated archipelago in the world, not near anywhere else. It is in the middle of the Pacific, almost 2,500 miles from California and slightly more than 4,000 miles from Japan. To ship onions takes too much storage time. In addition to the expense, it takes ten days to ship to the West Coast and the shelf life of a Kula onion is only a month. This is the problem with sweet onions everywhere. On the West Coast, the closest market, it is extremely difficult for Maui onions to compete with sweet onions from California or Walla Walla.

Maui is one of the few places in the world where onions can be grown all year. In the 1980s, Hawaiians began looking for summer varieties. Although fairly close to the equator, Hawaii still has slightly more than two and a half more hours of daylight in the summer than in the winter, and this is a different growing season. Haleakalā means "house of the sun," and there is a legend that the god Maui imprisoned the sun there in order to lengthen the day. Grano seeds were introduced to grow in the summer. Maui is one of the few places in the world where onions can be grown all year. So now there is variety in Kula onions: some are flat and some round. But they all must be grown in the less-than-400-acre Kula district known locally as zip code 96790. And, typical of Hawaii, they are probably the world's most expensive onions.

Most of the farmers have smallholdings. Louis Escobedo from the Philippines started in 2005 and farms only 5 acres in onions. He buys seeds and grows them to shoots, sets, which he plants every two weeks all year. He keeps his small plots refreshed by rotating them with bok choi, green peppers, or cabbage. Yet with a variety of seeds, he grows Kula onions all year round unless, as it occasionally happens, there is a rainy winter. But most years there is little rain on this part of the island, which is why the red landscape looks so barren.

Cornelio Cabaero, also from the Philippines, studied at the University of Hawaii before he decided to stay and plant onions on 45 acres in Kula. He rotates onions with zucchini crops, but he also, in a good year, produces onions all year. The work is all done by hand: two months in the seedbed, then transferred by hand to the field, then three to four more months before harvest. He harvests almost every month in one field or another with his wife, two of his five children, and two or three workers. Six people take a day to plant one acre. "Harvesting is the fun part of growing onions," he said. "If you have a good harvest you have a good future."

The onions are popular in Hawaii. The mild raw onion works well in Hawaiian dishes such as marinated fresh fish, poke. Louis Escobedo said that sometimes he likes to pick up an onion and eat it like an apple. "Just raw is very nice," he said.

Sweet onions are also grown in other countries, such as the Fuentes Sweet onion, *Cebolla Dulce de Fuentes*, near Zaragoza in Spain, and Cévennes onions in southeastern France. In Cévennes, one of the most picturesque and labor-intensive onion fields in the world, onions are planted on sandy terraced slopes of mountainsides, the small flat areas created with man-made walls to fight off erosion. The arduous labor of planting these terraces takes place starting in May. At the end of August is a three-week harvest, also by hand.

· · ·

Mr. Washington in his onion patch

Booker T. Washington, notable Black educator, working in his onion patch in Garden City, New York, in 1916.

Crossbreeding has developed a large variety of cepa onions. Names are not exact and vary from one country to another. The common round onion in the United States is called a Spanish onion. This supposes that it was the type the Spanish brought to the Americas, which may not be correct. Early Latin American recipes recommend the "Madeira" onion, which would be from Portugal. In any event, of all the many Spanish onions in the United States, not one comes from Spain. The United States does not import onions from Spain because it has so many of its own.

In the United States today, "Spanish onion" might be a Stockton Red Globe, Early Yellow Globe, Australian Brown, White Portugal, Southport Yellow Globe, Red Wethersfield, Southport Red Globe, Italian Red, or Flat Madeira. Other American onions include Granex, Grano, White Creole, Eclipse, California Early Red, Ebenezer, Early Strasburg, Yellow Globe Danvers, Yellow Flat Grant, Yellow Rynsburg, and Zittan Yellow.

Spain remains an important onion producer, especially in the province of Valencia, but these onions are mostly for Spain and the rest of Europe, particularly Britain. Locally, Valencianos, a Catalan-speaking people, put the onions over a fire in the orchards. Then they peel the blackened exterior and add salt, olive oil, and a touch of vinegar to the inner onions. Valencia, a stately city of Muslim and Christian origins, is surrounded by rich agricultural lands including onion fields and a system of canals, rice paddies, and waterways known as La Huerta. Paella comes from La Huerta. It originated as, and still is, a midday meal for farm workers. To Catalans, it is a faux pas to serve paella at night. Nor does the true paella have seafood. A paella is supposed to be made of the local produce from La Huerta, cooked with the local rice. This means onions and tomatoes and a flat bean related to a lima bean called a *garrofó*, and rabbit, sometimes duck, and sometimes chicken.

· · ·

The expression "no pain, no gain" is not always true in cooking, though it often is. There is a constant attempt to get the onion without paying the price, i.e., tears. That is why onion powder, ground dehydrated onions, was invented. It does not make you cry, but it does not make you sing. It does not have the strong flavor we love in onions. Some chefs find it useful for certain dishes, the same way Indian chefs sometimes use dry ground ginger. Paul Prudhomme, the late New Orleans chef, on occasion used onion powder in combination with fresh onions, saying that the combination could make "the final effect more balanced and interesting."

The claim of Bob Stafford in Vidalia that there will always be some bite because "an onion is an onion" may not always be true. Scientists in New Zealand and in Japan have been developing a new species that does not have the ability to produce tears. Scientist Eric Block reported that they had "a wonderful, fresh, sweet onion aroma." Supposedly it will be oniony without the pain. But will that be an onion?

Part Two

HOW TO EAT AN ONION

la tierra
asi te hizo,
cebolla,
claro como un planeta, y destinada
a relucir . . .

and so the earth
made you,
onion,
as bright as a planet and fated
to shine . . .

—PABLO NERUDA, "ODE TO THE ONION"

My long-standing fascination with historical recipes is partly a fascination with the people who wrote them. Cookbook authors are as interesting as recipes. They include novelists, social reformers, theologians, and politicians. Writing cookbooks was one of the few highly respected careers open to women and so the brightest and most capable women were drawn to it. Cookbook writers are among the early champions of women's rights.

All of this history becomes apparent in the history of onion recipes, because few food writers have overlooked the onion.

. . .

The all-important and often ignored way to begin is to choose the right onion. There is a lot more to consider than the shape, size, and color, though those are also important decisions. Whatever type of onion is used, the challenge is to use a good one. The first thing you are told is to look for a crisp, dry skin. This assumes that you are eating cured onions. My favorite onion treat is in the spring when farmers sometimes sell their first white onions out of the ground with fine, crisp greenery and bulbs too fresh to have grown a skin. The greens can be chopped up for salads, fish, or other seasoning, and the bulbs split in half vertically, sprinkled with olive oil and a little salt and broiled until the ring edges are brown. There is no better vegetable.

When selecting cured onions from the bin in a store, make sure they are of an even hardness with no soft spots and that the neck is completely closed. There should be no sprouting. The onion should have only a mild onion smell. Even if it is a strong onion, that should not be evident until it is cut.

Not surprisingly, there are many disagreements on the proper use of onions. Karl Friedrich von Rumohr, the great chronicler of German nineteenth-century cooking, claimed that the common practice of putting an onion in a beef stock was a mistake. "They impart a stale flavor when boiled."

It is often said that it is wrong to mix alliums in the same dish. But garlic and onions are traditional in the Mediterranean, and leeks and onions are favored in the north. In the French Caribbean, a stock begins with onions, shallots, and garlic. During the Middle Ages, when the English were passionate about alliums in their salad, a recipe sometimes called for onions, garlic, shallots, leeks, and also young leeks.

In the mid-nineteenth century, the English food writer Tabitha Tickletooth came to the aid of those criticized for eating raw onions. It may not surprise you to know that Tabitha Tickletooth was not a real name. The actor Charles Selby amused himself with the pseudonym, dressing as a woman, a housewife with a lacy bonnet and frilly apron and no attempt to hide his masculine face, and gave cooking advice to "fellow" housewives. An onion, Tabitha declared, "is one of the most useful and valuable friends of all our kitchens, where it constantly appears either openly in its native succulency and 'half-goût', or subdued and civilized by artful disguises."

Here are some of the leading disguises.

5

Onion Soup

The celebrated food writer M. F. K. Fisher, citing Georges-Auguste Escoffier as an example, opined that the best part of cookbooks is often the soup section. She called soups an "infinitely variable subject." And there is no more ubiquitous soup in cookbooks than onion soup.

Onion soup, perhaps because it is a most digestible way of enjoying the sweetness of onions, has always been accorded great significance. American novelist Willa Cather, in *Death Comes for the Archbishop*, depicts a priest, Bishop Latour, serving a French onion soup for Christmas dinner. He says that the soup is "not the work of one man. It is the result of a constantly refined tradition. There are nearly a thousand years of history in that soup." And there may be a thousand variations on it as well.

Onion soups, or at least recipes for them, first appeared in the Middle Ages. In England there was a dish called *Bruet de Almayne*, Middle English for German broth. Onions were chopped and sautéed in oil with cloves and cubebs, which are pepper-like berries of a shrub. It was simmered for a time in milk, almond milk if it was a holy day when dairy was forbidden. *Porrey chaplain* was a soup of pastry rings and sautéed sliced onions cooked in milk or almond milk. *Cherolace* was chopped onions cooked in a stock with saffron and cinnamon.

In France most districts have their own variation. In south-western France, the area known as Béarn *ouillat*, a simple onion soup is served with a splash of vinegar. This soup does not have cheese but sometimes garlic, tomatoes, and cheese are added—but then it is called *soupe du berger*, shepherd's soup.

Near Béarn, in Gascon, the traditional soup is *potage garbure*, which is made by sautéing onions and other vegetables in goose fat with salt-cured pork and goose. Garbure is covered with grated cheese, but since the cheese is not from the region, this may not have been part of the original recipe. The Provençal chef Jean-Baptiste Reboul, in his now-classic 1897 *La cuisinière proven-çale*, collected more than a thousand Provençal recipes. Most of them are worth considering, including this garbure recipe, which he correctly identified as from neighboring Gascon:

Mince 2 onions, 2 or 3 turnips, 3 or 4 potatoes, and a half cabbage. Put several spoonsful of rendered goose fat in a casserole. Add the onions, then the turnips, then the cabbage, and a few minutes later the potatoes, mix with 3 liters [slightly more than three quarts] of water. Add a piece of *petit ale blanc* [salt-cured pork belly, which is unsliced bacon] and let it cook.

When the pork is cooked, cut into thin slices and cut the same quantity of *oie confit* [salt-cured goose]. Cut thin slices of bread. Place a soup tureen over the fire and place alternating beds of bread, pork, and goose. Pour the soup over it and dust the top with grated cheese and put in the oven to melt the cheese.

In the same 1897 book, Reboul also gave a recipe for puréed onion soup:

Put 50 grams [slightly less than 2 ounces] of butter in a casserole with 4 or 5 minced onions, let them cook without browning. Add 2 full soup-spoons of flour [stir together first], then add 3 liters [slightly more than three quarts] of bouillon and let it cook, and then force it through a fine sieve and keep it warm. Add a well-blended 3 egg yolks with a glass of milk and a touch of grated nutmeg. And serve with small bread croutons fried in butter.

One of the oldest French onion soup recipes is from *Le Mesnagier de Paris*, a 1393 book in which an older man gives advice on a wide range of wifely subjects to a young woman. The book includes recipes, and one is for an onion soup. The onions are sliced and cooked in broth and then a puree of peas is added.

At the time of the French Revolution, Paris onion soup had bread but no cheese, at least according to the recipe of Paris's first food critic, Alexandre-Balthazar-Laurent Grimod de La Reynière, who more conveniently is known as Grimod de La Reynière, or even better, Grimod. Born on the Champs-Élysées to Parisian aristocrats, who seemed to always delight in very long names, he had horribly deformed hands and his parents kept him hidden. He rebelled when they left town, once hosting an all-night fourteen-course meal. Another time he hosted a dinner with a live pig dressed up as his father. Dad came home and was most unamused and sent his son off to an Augustine abbey, where he learned more about food and cooking.

After the revolution, starting in 1812, Grimod began publishing annual guides to food and Paris restaurants, creating the template for all future reviewers whose opinions would sanctify or destroy restaurants. Every Wednesday he would invite twelve friends and have food sent over and judged by the group. Eventually he became extremely unpopular, accused of taking bribes for good reviews. He pretended to die and staged his own funeral to see who would come. Almost no one, as it turned out. He left Paris for good and died at the age of 80 in 1837.

Grimod said that "soup is the prologue to a dinner," and offered this recipe for onion soup, which he attributed to his friend Louis, the Marquis de Cussy, who was the head steward in Napoleon's household, and celebrated for his recipes:

Take twenty small onions, peel them and cut them into thin slices. Put them in a pan with a knob of butter and a little sugar. Stir them until they are golden brown, then add a decent quantity of good stock and bread. Just before serving the soup, throw in a couple of small glasses of old Cognac.

They must have had a reason to believe that small onions were better, because large onions would have been much less work.

. . .

The most famous onion soup is from Paris, where it is made of onions cooked in broth with toasted bread and grated cheese. But neither of these embellishments originated in Paris. In 1844, Cora Millet-Robinet gave a recipe for onion soup that included both in her book *Maison rustique des dames* (*The French Country Housewife*), which was continually reprinted until 1944. Although born in Paris in 1798, in 1820 she and her husband, a retired soldier, moved to Poitou, on the Atlantic side of central France. A tireless political progressive in conservative rural France through the upheavals of the nineteenth century, Cora Millet-Robinet gave her book a distinctly feminist tone, offering advice for women on how to play a leading role in farm management and not merely be an appendage of the husband. She included tips on agriculture and cooking. Here is her onion soup, a flour-thickened vegetable soup or pottage, featuring bread and grated cheese, with variations that speak to the issue of whether or not an onion soup should be made with a stock:

Put some butter in a copper or iron saucepan, placed on a brisk fire. Peel and thinly slice one or several onions, according to how large they are and how much soup you wish to make. Add a half-spoonful of flour. Let them fry until they have all taken a nice color. Add the correct amount of water, preferably boiling, not cold, some salt, and a little pepper. Leave to boil for at least a quarter of an hour. Pour it all onto very thin slices of bread, which you have placed in a tureen to alternate layers of grated Parmesan or Gruyère cheese. You can strain the soup so as not to have any onion in the tureen.

One way to make this soup into an excellent pottage [pottages are heavier than soups] is to make it with a stock made from fresh-podded haricots; in this case do not add flour and the flavor is very similar to a soup made with meat stock. A broth made from lentils, broad beans, dried haricots, or French beans also makes something a great deal better. You can even add a puree made from the vegetables that served as a base for the broth. A little meat stock added to the water that you pour over the fried onions gives this soup an excellent flavor.

Though Cora Millet-Robinet believed in adding meat stock for flavor, Alexandre Dumas père did not. His *Grand dictionnaire de cuisine*, published in 1873, three years after his death, was a

Alexandre Dumas, 1847.

chaotic, possibly unfinished collection of recipes, but among the interesting ones is a recipe for onion soup with no meat stock.

Often shaky on food facts and history, Dumas always told a good story. This one begins:

> During one of his trips between Luneville and Versailles, where the ex-king of Poland, Stanislas, went each year to visit his daughter, the queen, he stopped at an inn in Châlons, where he was served a soup so delicate and perfectly prepared that he was unwilling to continue his journey without having learned how to prepare a similar one.
>
> Wrapped in his dressing gown, His Majesty descended to the kitchen . . .

This might have been the opening to a novel as rich and colorful as *The Count of Monte Cristo*, but it is actually just a prelude to the recipe for *Soupe à l'oignon à la Stanislas*:

Take off the top crust of a loaf of bread and break it into pieces, which are to be heated on both sides. When the crusts are hot, rub them with fresh butter, and put them once more near the fire until they are lightly roasted. Then put them on a plate while the onions are sautéed in fresh butter. Usually one uses 30 grams [1 ounce] of butter for three large onions, diced very small, which are left on the fire until they have taken on a beautiful, slightly dark, golden color, a color which is obtained only by almost constant stirring. Then add the crusts and continue to stir until the onions become brown, moisten them with boiling water to unstick them from the casserole, season as necessary, then leave them to simmer for at least a quarter of an hour before serving.

It is a mistake to think that this soup is improved by using bouillon; on the contrary, this addition makes it too rich and lessens its delicacy.

For Dumas, grating cheese on top apparently would also make the soup less delicate.

Though not a Paris original, onion soup is strongly tied to the city's culture. Paris is a city where people go out at night. In fact, sadly, cooking at home has fallen out of fashion.

While the French are famously early-to-bed people in the provinces, in Paris they stay out and drink and then can't get home, because the Métro stops running at 12:40 A.M. on weekdays and at 1:40 on Fridays and Saturdays, and doesn't start up again until 5:30. The way to end an evening of drink was to go to Les Halles market and have an onion soup. Many foods were available late at night there, but onion soup was considered the best way to sober up and so was referred to as *soupe d'ivrogne*, "drunkard's soup."

In 1971 Les Halles market was torn down and replaced with a charmless shopping mall. Parisians who could not afford a taxi still had the problem of the Métro closure. Certain cafés scattered throughout the city remain open all night for a distinctly working-class crowd trying to get back to the more affordable suburbs. Some sleep with their arms folded on the tables. Some have onion soup—and then sleep. At about 5 A.M., daybreak, they all pay up and leave for the Métro to go home.

Onion soup has other social functions in France. More in the provinces than in Paris, a newlywed couple has onion soup after their first night because, it is thought, the soup will restore them sexually.

Some years ago, when he was still a young and rebellious chef, I spoke to Alain Senderens about onion soup and many other topics over one of the best lunches I have ever eaten, at his Paris restaurant, Lucas Carton. I still remember the tastes and textures of his rouget with its liver and fried parsley leaves like emerald crystals on top. Senderens was one of the leading advocates of a leaner French cuisine. He was very fit looking and ran regularly. He said that if a chef was fat that was reason to be suspicious of his food.

According to Senderens, if you are eating onion soup to sober up, it is more effective without cheese. But no one would serve it that way in Paris. Here is his recipe for a *soupe à l'oignon* that serves four:

2 tablespoons butter

3 ounces grated Gruyère or Parmesan cheese

3 large onions, finely sliced

4 cups water or beef broth

Salt

4 slices country-style bread

Heat the butter in a heavy flameproof casserole over moderate heat. Add the onions and cook, stirring regularly, until the onions are well browned (but not burned!). Add the water or broth, cover the casserole, and simmer for 30 minutes. Set each piece of bread in a soup bowl. Cover each slice with a quarter of the cheese (if desired) and pour the hot soup over both. Should you add cheese to the soup, be careful not to add too much salt.

VARIATION: Toast the bread (it can be lightly buttered or rubbed with garlic), cover with the cheese, and melt the cheese under a broiler. Set these pieces of bread on top of the soup. You can also add a little white wine or port to the soup (if your goal is not sobriety).

. . .

Though the Paris classic has ended up a huge influence every-where, onion soup evolved differently in other countries. In fifteenth-century England, *Kalendare de Potage Dyvers* offered a recipe for an onion soup with almonds. A dorrye was a soup with a golden color, often from egg yolks or saffron, but in this case it was almonds that gave the color. This soup was topped with slices of toast with toasted almonds. This soup dorrye, from the fifteenth-century manuscript, in a recipe that is difficult to decipher, may have been of French origin, especially with the use of olive oil and wine. It was collected in the twentieth century by Maxime de la Falaise, a highborn British woman who became a fashion model, the intimate of famous artists, fled Europe a diag-nosed kleptomaniac, and then became a food writer for *Vogue*:

Nym [take] and mince them small and fry them in oil d'olif—Nym wine and boil it with the onions toast whit bread and do it in dishes and good almond milk also and do them about and serve forth.

Hannah Glasse was a dominant figure in eighteenth-century British cooking. Her books were so popular, her name so well known, that Dr. Johnson opined that Hannah Glasse must be a made-up figure whose books were actually compiled by one or several men. This was an odd claim, since it was not unusual for women to compile recipes. But it was unusual for a woman to be this successful. It did not help her that she followed the modest approach of many women authors of the time, not signing her name but simply stating on the cover that the book was "by a Lady." But as with many other books signed "by a Lady," the author's identity was quickly discovered, perhaps because the authors had no real desire to remain hidden.

Today, food historians value Hannah Glasse for two reasons. The first is that she thoroughly documented a pre-industrial British cuisine that could hold its own compared to French. In fact, Glasse showed a notable distaste for French cooking. The second is that like those of many cookbook authors, her recipes

Hannah Glasse, 1777.

were not original, so when you see a Hannah Glasse recipe, you know this was a dish that was frequently made in this period.

There is something joyfully physical about Glasse's recipes, the way butter sizzles till it stops making noise, the way food is "thrown" into the pot, or the way you shake in a little flour. This approach to language was adopted by other recipe writers well into the next century. And while the dishes themselves were nothing new to eighteenth-century readers, today they offer a glimpse at a nearly forgotten cuisine before two centuries of industrial food took over. This onion soup recipe is from her 1747 book, *The Art of Cookery Made Plain and Easy*. Without cheese, thickened with eggs, and spiced with vinegar, the soup was a far cry from the Parisian one we think of today:

Take half a Pound of Butter, put it into a Stew-pan on the Fire, let it all melt, and boil till it has done making any Noise: then have ready ten or a Dozen middling Onions peeled, and cut small, throw them into the butter, and let them fry a quarter of an Hour, then shake in a little Flour, and stir them round; shake your Pan and let them do a few Minutes longer, then pour in a Quart or three Pints of boiling Water, stir them round, take a good Piece of Upper-crust, the stalest bread you have, about as big as the Top of a Penny-loaf cut small, and throw it in, season with Salt to your Palate, let it boil ten Minutes, stirring it often; then take it off of the Fire, and have ready the Yolks of two eggs beat fine, with half a Spoonful of Vinegar, Mix some of the Soop with them, then stir it into your Soop, and mix it well, and pour it into your Dish. This is a delicious Dish.

Only a few years later, in 1753, an anonymous British book, *The Lady's Companion: Containing upwards of three thousand different receipts in every kind of cookery: and those the best and most fashionable; being four times the quantity of any book of this sort,* instructed readers to make onion soup with milk. This British book also enjoyed popularity in some American colonies, despite calling its onion soup "The King's Soup," suggesting that it was a favorite of King George II:

> Take some onions cut in very thin slices, stew them till tender in a small quantity of water, then add milk, let it all boil together, at least half an hour. With a pretty many blades of mace, and a quarter pound of fresh butter, a little before it is taken up, thicken it with the yolks of two eggs well beaten, and some parsley, picked and chopped very small; salt to your taste. Serve it up with toast cut in dice.
>
> About four large onions will do to two quarts milk.

This recipe has problems. There was a tendency at the time to call any cooking in liquid "boiling," whereas a better word in this case might be simmering. Boiling would be too hot for the milk, scalding it, and to avoid curdling, the egg yolks would have to be introduced at a very moderate temperature, probably off the heat.

The first onion soups in America came from English books, especially from the anonymous *Lady's Companion,* also titled *The Ladies Companion,* published the same year by F. Hodges and R. Baldwin. The Hodges and Baldwin edition may have been the more influential in America; it was in Martha Washington's

collection. It gives this recipe for onion soup with milk—
remarkably similar to Hannah Glasse's, but without eggs:

> Take some Onions cut in very thin Slices. Stew them till
> tender, in a small Quantity of Water, then add Milk, let it all
> boil together, at least half an Hour, with a pretty many Blades
> of Mace.

Only a few years later, in 1759, William Verrall, a French-
trained English cook working in Sussex, published a book to
introduce French cuisine to the British. While Glasse was
trying to assert the Britishness of local cooking, Verrall was
doing the opposite, trying to make British food more French.
His onion soup, which he calls in slightly mangled Franglais
potage aux onions, is a clear broth as in France and includes
toast and/or cheese. But then there is that surprising chunk of
meat:

> It differs from a clear gravy, before prescribed only in this,
> take three or four large onions, take off the second coat and
> slice them in halves very thin, lay them in water awhile, dry
> them and fry them of a nice brown, in a bit of fresh butter,
> pour in a little warm water, and strain 'em upon a sieve that
> they may not be greasy; put them into your soup to boil a few
> minutes, order your crusts as before, put to the bottom of
> your dish, pour your soup in, and serve it up with a knuckle
> of veal or without as you like best. Very small onions are
> sometimes used for a change; fried in the same manner,
> whole.

By 1829, the pseudonymous Mistress Dods's *Cook and House-wife's Manual* offered a number of onion soups. One suggestion was to sauté chopped onions in butter and mix them with "a very strong stock-broth, add pepper, cayenne, and salt," and then, "if nicer cooking is wanted, strain the soup and add to it a pint of boiling cream." She suggested a number of other alternatives, such as using button onions instead of chopped large ones. She also had a number of proposals to "heighten the gusto," such as adding curry powder or ginger or mushroom catsup, a popular condiment before tomatoes came to dominate. Dods never specified the amount of onions in her recipes because tastes vary, and she made the interesting but to my knowledge unproven observation that "the taste for onions, like that for olives and peppers, increases with age."

Isabella Mary Beeton, a London writer who became famous for her 1861 *Book of Household Management*, included an onion soup from the same tradition with cream. Though she died at the age of twenty-eight of a fever following childbirth, her book was tremendously influential and remains in print. She was frequently criticized for her lack of originality, and some of her recipes, such as her "cheap onion soup" made with rice flour and sugar, seem awful. But others, such as the onion soup recipe with cream, are excellent:

Ingredients—6 large onions, 2 ounces of butter, salt and pepper to taste, ¼ pint of cream, 1 quart of stock [her stock includes beef, veal knuckle, poultry, bacon, and large onions studded with cloves, mace, turnips and carrots; a good stock is the key to this soup].

Mode—chop the onions, put them in the butter, stir them occasionally, but do not let them brown. When tender, put the stock to them, and season, strain the soup and add the boiling cream.

It seems likely that she meant for five of the onions to be chopped, and the sixth, studded with spices, to be cooked whole.

In Iberia, there has always been more interest in garlic soup, an Arab dish that is common throughout Spain and has remained especially popular in Andalusia, the southern region that was Arab-ruled for centuries.

But in Iberian regions closer to France, onion soup is often part of the cuisine, especially in the Basque province of Guipúzcoa. There, Basques gather in private cooking clubs that preserve the local recipes. The gastronomic club Txirikil in Eibar has among its recipes one for an onion soup similar to the French version, only without the cheese and with a healthy shot of Cognac, which is not a local product.

In San Sebastián, a Basque city that Napoleon's occupation left with considerable French influences, Felix Ibarguren, a famous Basque known popularly as Shishito, established this gastronomic capital's first cooking school in 1901, and defined San Sebastián cooking at the turn of the century. He made an onion soup that had the same Gruyère cheese that is made in Switzerland far from Guipúzcoa and is featured on French soups. But he also included potatoes.

Henri Charpentier was born in Nice in 1880 and went on to cook for and later supervise some of the most famous restaurants in the world, including the Savoy in London and Delmonico's in New York. In 1948, he opened his own fourteen-seat restaurant in Redondo Beach, south of Los Angeles, where reservations had to be made more than a year in advance. He cooked for the rich and famous, and his most celebrated invention was crêpe suzette, which he made for the British royal family who were dining with someone named Suzette. He also offered traditional Paris-style onion soup, although made with red onions and, to please President Theodore Roosevelt, he made it with Parmesan cheese rather than Gruyère. In his memoir, *Those Rich and Great Ones, or Life à la Henri,* he wrote at length about his relationship with Roosevelt and about the Teddy onion soup. Henri was also one of the last to write a recipe really well:

> Invariably, I think, he wanted onion soup. The first time he came he was dubious because he thought mine would not be so good as some he had eaten in France.
>
> The way to make it, Henri style, is to slice, on the bias, three red onions previously peeled. I put these slices in a casserole containing a tablespoon of hot butter. Into this bland substance the onions surrender all their juice. Properly this should be accomplished over a slow fire. This part of the process is complete when the onion slices have turned the color of gold. Three onions, I find, are sufficient to provide the flavor for soup for two persons; four may make sufficient for four or five, but for myself, when I am hungry, I want six onions. Henri wants his onion soup thick, but even I want them well cooked. The

breath of a raw onion is completely uncivilized; but a thoroughly cooked onion, remember, leaves you inoffensive, even desirable.

When your onions have turned the proper color then you add to them about a quart of cold chicken or beef consommé. Now permit this to boil thoroughly; between a half and three quarters of an hour. The final action is to toast a slice or two of bread or a handful of croutons and then in the heat of your oven melt on these grated Parmesan or Swiss cheese. Launch these cheese-laden rafts gently on the boiling hot soup, cover the pot and then place it in the oven for ten minutes. This part of the process gives to the soup the flavor of the cheese. It is, therefore, most important. When you serve send along as an escort a saucer of grated Parmesan for the use of those whose taste is less delicate than yours and mine.

"Henri," said Mr. Roosevelt many times, "I think I like your onion soup better than that I have eaten in France."

Well, I myself do not say it is better. I am content to know it is as good.

Originally known as the Southern Branch of the Union Pacific, in 1865 the line became the Missouri-Kansas-Texas Railway, popularly known as the Katy (as in K T). In the 1930s, T. T. Turner, superintendent for dining service on the Katy, invented the Katy Onion Soup to popularize Texas onions, a newly expanding Texas product. At first it was not well received, but in time most passengers, nine out of ten, according to one report, were asking for Katy Onion Soup. This is Turner's recipe, but originally he always specified Texas onions:

6 large onions, ⅛ inch diced
4 ounces butter
4 quarts rich chicken stock
4 sprigs parsley
1 clove garlic
2 bay leaves
¼ cup Worcestershire sauce
soup croutons
Parmesan cheese, freshly grated

Slice onions ⅛ inch thick, then dice. In the large skillet over medium heat, sauté onion in butter until light brown. Meanwhile, heat stock in pot. Add sautéed onions to heated stock. Add parsley, garlic, bay leaves, and Worcestershire sauce. Bring to a boil, reduce heat, and simmer for 20 minutes. Remove parsley, bay leaves, and garlic. Place croutons in serving bowls, pour soup over, and top with a generous portion of freshly grated Parmesan cheese.

. . .

In Japan, onion soup, or *negi-jiru*, has a different meaning. As with much of Japanese cooking, the soup's main feature is not the onions, though they are prominent. In Japan, green onions commonly partner with fish, and so in Osaka there is *negi-ma-jiru*, onion tuna soup. In Japan there are as many cuts of tuna as there are cuts of beef in the West. Traditionally this soup was made with toro—the fatty tender cut from the belly. Now that sushi has become more upscale than it used to be, toro has become extremely expensive and since this soup was not intended to be deluxe, it is often made with a lesser cut today. Also, it would be a good idea to avoid the endangered bluefin tuna, so loved and so slaughtered in Japan, and use other species.

This recipe comes from Shizuo Tsuji, who died in 1993 and had been the head of Japan's leading school for professional chefs in Osaka. Among the many interesting tidbits of his colorful life—his culinary accomplishments, his degree in French litera-ture, his journalism career—the one that always fascinated me is that he owned one of the world's most extensive collections of Bach recordings. This is his recipe for negi-ma-jiru:

1 pound raw tuna [the fattier the better]
10 green onions
4 cups dashi [a broth made from seaweed; can be bought or made]
¾ teaspoon salt
1 tablespoon light soy sauce
shichimi [a peppery Japanese seven-spice blend; can be bought]
To prepare: Cut the raw tuna cross wise against the grain into slices about ¼ inch thick, and then cut the slices into 1-inch pieces. Lay tuna pieces in a colander and pour boiling water over them (or plunge into boiling water); immediately rinse under cold water.

Cut the green onions diagonally into 1 ½-inch lengths.

To cook and serve: In a medium-sized pot combine the dashi, salt, and soy sauce and bring to a simmer. Add the tuna, and simmer, just on the verge of boiling (do not boil), for about

2 minutes. Add the onion and stir. Immediately remove from heat.

Ladle into soup bowls and sprinkle with a scant amount of seven spice (*shichimi*) mixture. Serve immediately.

. . .

I could not finish the onion soup section without mentioning Louis Diat's Vichyssoise, my childhood favorite, possibly still my favorite.

Vichyssoise, a celebrated dish in twentieth-century cuisine, is not as popular as it once was. Though invented by a Frenchman, it is actually a New York dish and not French. Instead, it was the inspiration of Diat, who moved to New York in 1910, became a U.S. citizen, and worked for forty-one obsessive, workaholic years as the chef of the Ritz-Carlton Hotel. Each summer he tried to invent a cold soup for the hot months in New York, and in 1917 he came up with a *"crème vichyssoise glacée."* Diat said he was

Louis Diat, 1926.

inspired by his childhood memories of the area near Vichy. And there, the French do make an onion-potato-leek soup, though it is usually not chilled.

As a child I loved everything about this soup—its presentation and taste, the way it was served in a metal bowl sitting on a dish of shaved ice, the coldness of both the bowl and the soup, the thick creaminess of the soup as I moved my spoon through it, and those bright green random dashes of chives. With its onions, leeks, and chives it is an allium celebration. It was served at my parents' favorite Hartford restaurant, the Hearthstone, and at several New York restaurants as well, always with this same presentation. This is Diat's recipe from his 1941 book, *Cooking a la Ritz*:

4 leeks, white part
1 medium onion
2 ounces sweet butter
5 medium potatoes
1 quart water or chicken broth
1 tablespoon salt
2 cups milk
2 cups medium cream
1 cup heavy cream
Finely slice the white part of the leeks and the onion, and brown very lightly in the sweet butter, then add the potatoes, also sliced finely. Add water or broth and salt. Boil from 35 to 40 minutes. Crush and rub through a fine strainer. Return to fire and add two cups of milk and 2 cups of medium cream. Season to taste and bring to a boil. Cool and then rub through

a very fine strainer. When soup is cold add the heavy cream. Chill thoroughly before serving. Finely chopped chives may be added when serving.

Diat also made a traditional Paris onion soup with toast and grated cheese. His only variation was the addition of peeled chopped tomatoes, which he viewed as an optional ingredient.

History shows that if you throw some onions in a pot with something else, you get a good soup.

6

Sauces

Onion sauces, once entrenched in many cultures, seem to have fallen from favor. Most general cookbooks in past centuries offered at least one, often several onion sauce recipes.

On Michaelmas Day, September 29, the feast of St. Michael in Britain and Ireland, a roast goose is so traditional that the holiday is sometimes called "Goose Day." The harvest was in and financial accounts were settled. The goose was left to forage in the harvested fields and was now a symbol of good fortune. Though in Ireland today the goose is more commonly served with applesauce, in the eighteenth century it was always served with onion sauce. The onions were cooked in a pot of half milk and half water until they were soft. Often a slice of turnip was included, which was supposed to draw off some of the edge from the onions. Then the onions (and turnip, if added) were mashed with butter, nutmeg, black pepper, and salt. Sometimes some cream was added and reduced until thickened.

In her 1974 book, *English Food*, British food writer Jane Grigson, who died in 1990, wrote that the traditional boiled salted duck of the Isle of Man was always to be served with an onion sauce. She suggested a sauce recipe from the Isle of Man in which chopped onions and corn flour are cooked in milk while stirring until thickened and then fresh lemon rind is added for seasoning.

Godey's Lady's Book, the most popular women's magazine of mid-nineteenth-century America, with 150,000 readers in both the North and the South during the Civil War, offered this recipe for onion sauce in 1862:

> Boil the onions until tender, changing the water occasionally to render them more mild. Strain and mash the onions in a bowl, adding butter and salt. Warm up again and mix the whole thoroughly.

This is a nineteenth-century sweet caraway onion sauce for lamb roasts from Elena Molokhovets's *A Gift to Young Housewives*:

> Slice 5–6 onions, add 3 glasses boiling bouillon, boil, and rub through a sieve. Lightly fry 1 spoon flour in 2 spoons butter [melt the butter and blend in the flour], dilute with a glass of bouillon, boil thoroughly and strain. Mix the sauce with 2

glasses of the strained onion purée, add 1 ½ teaspoons of caraway seeds and some caramelized sugar, and bring to a boil several times.

The issue of onion sauce had already been settled by the French and most followed their lead. After the French Revolution and into the twentieth century, French cooking became codified into something known as Classic French Cuisine. This had little to do with home cooking, though at times it influenced it. The beginnings were after the French Revolution when guilds began to fade and chefs were free to create. Particularly in Paris, a style of cuisine for the wealthy gourmet became fashionable. Marie-Antoine Carême dominated, creating hundreds of recipes, prescribing an exact formula for dishes. It was a cuisine that required a huge, highly trained kitchen staff of specialists. Classic French Cuisine was aspired to by many but achieved by only a few. Later Georges-Auguste Escoffier, chef, writer, and owner of a number of famous restaurants, simplified and modernized the cuisine. Modern cooks are astounded by his motto, "Make it simple," because his recipes were elaborate and often complicated. Still, they were simpler than Carême's.

Sauces were a demanding craft in themselves, and a restaurant maintained a full staff of sauce makers. There were hundreds of sauces, and many of them started with other sauces. Sauces such as *espagnole* and *béchamel* were essential ingredients in making other sauces. You cannot make a classic *sauce soubise* without béchamel, and sauce soubise was to become the definitive onion sauce, demonstrating the importance of Classic French Cuisine.

A. ESCOFFIER

Escoffier, 1910.

Onion sauce in a number of cultures had long been a thick, creamy white sauce with onions. Sauce soubise defined the "proper" creamy onion sauce, and most later onion sauces, with various degrees of success, copied it. Though associated with Escoffier's recipe, sauce soubise had been around before him. There are mentions of the sauce dating to the early 1870s, when Escoffier was a little-known chef in the French Army during the Franco-Prussian War, and it was said to have been named for Charles de Rohan, Prince of Soubise (1715–1787). It is not known why. Soubise was a prerevolutionary figure, an advisor to Louis XVI. Here is Escoffier's recipe for *Sauce Soubise*:

Mince 500 grams [about 1 pound] onions and blanch them well [plunge into boiling water for a few seconds]. After having thoroughly drained them, simmer them in butter and then add a half liter [about 4 cups] thick Béchamel sauce, a pinch of fine salt, a turn of white pepper, and a big pinch of powdered sugar. Cook slowly in the oven, pass through a sieve. Heat up the sauce with 80 grams [about 5 tablespoons] of butter and a decaliter [½ cup] of cream.

The trick here is to make a good béchamel. Many modern variations use shortcuts, which lead to clunky or pasty results, whereas a true béchamel is subtle and elegant. Béchamel was first mentioned in the early eighteenth century as a sauce for fish shortly after the death of Louis de Béchameil, the financier who was fated to forevermore have his name misspelled—assuming the sauce really was named after him. Carême's classic version in his 1817 *L'Art de la cuisine française* took most of a day for one of his sauce specialists to make. Just to make the correct stock from the proper assortment of meats was a major endeavor. Escoffier, the simplifier, outraged some by saying that his béchamel would only take an hour with a simple veal stock. After that hour you could begin the onion soubise. A roux—butter thickened with flour—has to be made first, and then a veal stock is made with onions and thyme, salt, and nutmeg, then milk must be boiled and the stock and the roux added. Despite his claim, this will undoubtedly take more than an hour. And that is just the base to make the onion sauce. A modern cook could buy a veal stock, add it to the boiling milk, and stir it into the roux until thickened.

There have been only a few variations on onion sauce. The rebel Margaret Dods, who wrote her *Cook and Housewife's Manual* during Carême's lifetime, boiled the onions, chopped them, then pureed them by forcing them through a sieve before sautéing. She only suggested adding cream for certain dishes, such as rabbit or duck, although she did mention that the French made onion sauce with béchamel.

Dods offered the alternative of a brown onion sauce, and a half century later, Agnes Bertha Marshall offered both a brown and a white onion sauce. Marshall was Victorian England's equivalent to a celebrity chef with books, well-attended talks and cooking demonstrations, and lots of products to sell. This is her brown onion sauce from her 1887 cookbook, *Mrs. A. B. Marshall's Cookery Book*:

Cut up six good size onions in slices, put them in a stew pan, to cover them, with enough cold water with a pinch of salt. Let them come to a boil. Strain off, wash with cold water, put them in a clean stew pan, add one ounce of fine flour, mix all together with half a pint of brown stock, and three quarters of a pint of brown sauce, and boil for about half an hour; add a dessertspoonful of white tarragon vinegar, a few drops of Marshall's carmine [her own red food-coloring product], and a dust of coralline pepper [powdered pink peppercorns], then pass the whole through the tammy [a fine cloth for straining sauces], boil up again, and use hot.

Alexis Soyer was a French chef who became famous in England for his attempts to feed the hungry in the Irish famine and to develop better field kitchens for British troops in the Crimean War. His 1854 *Soyer's Shilling Cookery for the People*, one of his books on budget-minded cooking, has the enticing addition of chopped sage to a standard onion sauce. Dods had also suggested adding sage to onion sauce. (Note that milk used to have a higher cream content than it has today, so when given the choice between milk or cream in a nineteenth-century recipe, always choose cream.)

Soyer starts with his "sauce foundation":

One ounce of butter, one and a half of flour, a little more salt, and pepper and a gill [a quarter of a pint] of water . . .

And then goes on to the next steps:

Boil four onions in salt and water, take them out, chop them up, and add them to the above with a little more salt, and a tablespoon of sugar, and a little milk or cream.
To the above, a tablespoonful of chopped green sage and a little more pepper.

In 1885, the thirty-two women of the Christian Woman's Exchange in New Orleans published a recipe book called *Creole Cookery*. This is their onion sauce recipe, which renders a thick and rich sauce. Creole is never about light.

Take 1 dozen onions, boil them till quite tender, with a little salt in the water; take them out and chop them fine, then stew them in a small quantity of sweet cream.

Under Jewish dietary law, an onion sauce when used for meat cannot have any dairy. This is the recipe from *The Jewish Manual*, edited by Lady Judith Cohen Montefiore, from 1846:

Slice finely, and brown in a little oil, two or three onions; put
them in a little beef gravy and add cayenne pepper, salt, and
the juice of a lemon. This is a nice sauce for steaks.

Jacques Médecin, the mayor of Nice from 1966 to 1990 and
later jailed for corruption, was also the author of a celebrated
book on the cuisine of the region. This is his recipe for a Niçoise
onion sauce or condiment, called in the dialect of Nice, *li céba
en samoira*, which means "marinated onions":

For six servings
1 kilo (2.2 pounds) little onions or quartered onions
2 lemons
10 sprigs of parsley
2 garlic cloves
150 grams of Malaga raisins (soaked for about an hour)
4 pinches of thyme leaves
½ bay leaf
1 teaspoon coriander seeds
1 glass dry white wine
2 tablespoons wine vinegar
2 tablespoons sugar
olive oil
salt
1 teaspoon black peppercorn
1. Heat six tablespoons of olive oil in a skillet. When the oil
begins to smoke add the onions until they turn white and
then add all above ingredients.

2. Let it sizzle, cover and sauté and let cook vigorously under the lid.

3. When it is reduced to half remove the lid and cook until it becomes thick.

Raisins are common in Mediterranean cooking and usually denote a Jewish origin to the dish, although that is not certain in this case.

.   .   .

Swiss-born Oscar Tschirky, maître d'hôtel of the Waldorf and of Delmonico's before that, was one of the most influential restaurateurs of New York's Gilded Age. In his 1896 *Cook Book by "Oscar" of the Waldorf* he offers three onion sauces, two of which are fairly standard, but then there is his "Onion Sauce with Vinegar":

Peel three good-sized onions, mince them fine, place them over the fire with a lump of butter and fry over a brisk fire until brown. Sift a tablespoonful of flour over the onions, pour two gills of water and season with salt, pepper, mustard, and vinegar to taste. Stir the sauce over the fire and boil until quite smooth. It is then ready for use.

Tschirky recommends his onion sauces for "roasted or boiled shoulder of mutton, tripe, ducks, or rabbit"—which demonstrates why one doesn't see onion sauces very often today. Who eats a shoulder of mutton?

7

Boiled, Braised, Roasted, and Stuffed

A boiled onion is an old idea for an inexpensive meal. This recipe comes from a 1597 English book by Thomas Dawson, *The Good Huswifes Jewell.* The boiled onions can be served with a sauce or in a soup with eggs on top.

To boile Onions: Take a good many onions and cut them in four quarters, set them on the fire in as much water as you think will boyle them tender and when they be clean skinned, put in a good many raisons, half a spoonful of grose pepper, a good peece of sugar, and a little salt, and when the onions be thorough boiled, beat the yolks of an egg with Vergious [verjus—sour grape juice] and put into your pot so serve it upen soppes [upon soups]. If you will, poach Eggs and lay upon them.

The challenge was to enjoy the sweet flavor of onions without the pungency. As Mrs. L. G. Abell wrote in her 1846 book, *The Complete Domestic Guide*:

It is well to boil onions in milk and water, to diminish their strong taste. They require an hour or more, and then press out the water a little, and season them with a little salt, pepper, and a little melted butter. They should be served hot with baked or roasted meat.

If you really were to boil onions in milk for an hour, the milk would be curdled and there would be little left of the onions. She could mean simmer, but still, an hour would be a bit too long. Slowly for fifteen minutes on a low heat would work better.

Mrs. J. Chadwick puts it more simply in her 1853 book, *Home Cookery*, published in Boston:

To Plain Boil Onions
Take off one skin and boil them half or three quarters of an hour. When taken up, put off another skin, and lay pieces of butter over the onions.

Marjorie Kinnan Rawlings, a novelist who, though born in Washington, D.C., and educated in Wisconsin, became associated with southern culture, recommended braised onions, which were boiled, then simmered with sugar and butter. Italian refugee Giacomo Castelvetro, attempting to educate the English on vegetables in a book published in 1614, wrote that when green onions were not available for a salad, roasted white onions with crushed black pepper worked well. He believed that roasting onions was "tastier and more wholesome than eating them boiled."

In 1699, the English writer John Evelyn, without having traveled to Italy, opined that in Italy "honest, laborious, countrymen" had improved on the British peasant's raw onion and bread. "With good bread, salt, and a little parsley, will make a contented meal with a roasted onion."

In the fifteenth century, Platina thought the rawness of onions needed to be corrected and advised in his book *On Right Pleasure and Good Health*:

> Onion is cooked under ash and cinders until it has breathed out all rawness. When it has cooled, it is cut up in bits, put on a plate and recommended rolled in salt, oil, and condensed must, or must [unfermented wine]. Some even sprinkle pepper or cinnamon on onions.

While roasted onions are usually made with large onions, in India, roasted onions, or *bhone piaz*, are made from thick slices. They are placed in a cast-iron skillet of smoking hot oil and tossed only for two or three minutes so that they still have some crispness. They are usually served with tandoori chicken, a popular modern dish based on an ancient technique of cooking in a clay pot.

One of the most influential cookbooks of nineteenth-century America, *Miss Leslie's Directions for Cookery*, which had sixty editions between 1837 and 1870, recommended that onions be parboiled before roasting.

. . .

Stuffed onions, and stuffed foods in general, are a Jewish tradition for the harvest festival of Sukkot because they symbolize an abundant harvest. But many cultures have stuffed onions in their cuisine.

Stuffing calls for the largest onions available. The onions must first be boiled or braised. Louis Diat said braised, and though he offered a simple stuffing, the preparation involved in braising them was elaborate. Braising, an almost forgotten art, rewards the patient:

Peel, parboil in boiling salted water. Place slices of fat salt pork in a saucepan with 1 slice of onion. Place the Spanish onion on them with slices of salt pork on top. Add a good meat gravy or broth. Bring to a boil and let cook slowly, well covered, in a moderate oven, about 30 to 40 minutes. When cooked, remove the slices of salt pork and baste the onions with meat extract [or glace de viande] until they are golden brown. Add a glass of sherry and serve with their own gravy.

This dish is a delight in itself, but Diat also used it in his recipe for stuffed onions:

Parboil large Spanish onions for 5 minutes. Remove the inner part and chop it. Add to this chopped onion, some chopped mushrooms and chopped parsley. Stuff the onions with this mixture and braise them as for Braised Onions (above). Serve with gravy. Stuffing can also be made of spinach, risotto, etc.

In *Mrs. A. B. Marshall's Cookery Book*, Agnes Bertha Marshall offered an unusually rich recipe for stuffed onions, which she called "Onions Farced à la Banville." Here they are fried:

Blanch some medium-sized Spanish onions and put them in a saucepan with enough light stock to cover them, and boil them till tender; take them up and stamp out the insides, as if coring them, with a plain round cutter about one to one and a half inches in diameter; season with salt and coralline pepper [ground pink peppercorns], fill up the insides of the onions with a farce prepared as below, and then sprinkle them over with flour and egg, breadcrumb them, and fry them in clean, boiling fat for about ten minutes. Rub the pieces that were taken from the centers of the onion through a wire sieve, and add a pat of butter, a little coralline pepper, and salt, two raw yolks of eggs, four tablespoons of cream or milk, and stir together in the bain marie [a large pot of softly simmering water into which another pot can be placed for mild cooking, something like a double boiler, usually to prevent the curdling of a custard] till the mixture thickens, then turn it out on to a hot dish; place the onions onto the top of this purée, and serve at once. Use the stock these were cooked in for soup purposes.

For farcing six onions, take six blanched game or poultry livers, remove the gall from them, and chop them up very fine, mix them with two chopped eschalots [shallots] and a quarter of a pound of chopped up cooked white meat, such as rabbit, chicken, veal, or pork, four raw chopped button mushrooms, a tablespoonful of chopped herbs, and a little coralline pepper and salt; put all these into a sauté pan and sauté for about five minutes, then mix with two ounces of freshly made white breadcrumbs and one whole egg, mix together and use. This would be sufficient to serve twelve people.

Mrs. J. Chadwick had also included a recipe for fried stuffed onions in her 1853 cookbook, but rather than frying them in deep fat like Marshall, she sautéed them in butter. Also, unlike Mrs. Marshall, Mrs. Chadwick's popularity, like that of many of the leading American cookbook writers, came from keeping recipes simple. She called this recipe "in the Brazilian style." It should also be noted that this recipe was from a time before meat grinders ruined so many dishes. This meat here is finely chopped—minced—not ground:

Peel the onions and force out the cores, after having parboiled them a little; fill the opening with minced meat; beat up an egg and glaze the opening on both sides where the meat was put in that it may not drop out. Then fry the onions whole, in butter.

The Countess Emilia Pardo Bazán also fried her stuffed onions. The wealthy aristocrat, born in 1851 in the Galician port of La Coruña in northwestern Spain, was not only a well-known writer by her midtwenties, at a time when few Spanish women gained such distinction, she also became, in 1916, the first woman to receive a chair at a Spanish university—the Central University of Madrid. She was also an outspoken champion of women's rights. After numerous notable works of fiction and nonfiction, she published a cookbook, *La cocina española antigua*, old-time Spanish cooking, in 1913. Here is her recipe for stuffed onions:

This is a nutritious and very enjoyable dish.

Look for large onions, cleaned, and drained. From the top clear out an area for stuffing.

The stuffing is composed of breadcrumbs soaked in milk, squeezed, two hard-boiled egg yolks, some grated cheese, finely chopped parsley, onion, salt and pepper. This all should be very well mixed.

Fill the onions with this mixture. Dust the onions with flour, and coat in egg yolks and fry them. Then sprinkle with vinegar.

Hungarian stuffed onions, with all the richness for which Hungarian food is infamous, are baked. This is the notable Hungarian-American restaurateur George Lang's recipe for *Töltött hagyma halasi módra*, which in Hungarian, one of the least comprehensible languages to outsiders, means "stuffed onions in the style of Halas." Halas, or Kishunhalas, is a town south of Budapest. The name means "fish," of which there used to be many in the neighboring lakes.

10 medium-sized Bermuda onions
¼ pound lard
1 pound cooked lean veal diced
1 garlic clove mashed
1 tablespoon minced flat parsley
1 teaspoon salt
½ pound double smoked bacon
1 cup sour cream
pinch of paprika
pinch of black pepper

1. Peel onions. Cut off tops in such a way that you can take out almost the entire center of each onion. Leave 2 or 3 layers remaining as a shell to contain the stuffing. Set aside the center of 1 onion. (Use the rest for another recipe.)

2. Cook onion shells in lightly salted water for about 10 minutes. Make sure they do not get too soft, because they must not collapse later. Drain onion shells and gently pat dry.

3. Chop enough of the reserved onion center to have about ¼ cup. Slowly wilt chopped pieces in most of the lard. Save 1 teaspoon lard to grease the baking dish.

4. Add diced veal, mashed garlic, parsley and salt. Cook the stuffing, uncovered, over very low heat. Add a few tablespoons of water when the mixture becomes dry. Finally there should be no liquid left when testing with a fork indicates that the veal is cooked.

5. Cool the stuffing mixture, then grind it. Fill the cooked onion shells with the mixture.

6. Cut the bacon into two-inch squares to fit over the tops of onions.

7. Grease a baking-serving dish with lard and place stuffed onions in it. Pour or spoon sour cream on top of the onions. Sprinkle a little paprika and black pepper on each.
8. Place onions in a 350-degree F oven and bake for 25 to 30 minutes. Serve as a hot appetizer or a luncheon dish.

For an elaborate stuffed onion, though, the Russians may even outdo the Hungarians. Here is Elena Molokhovets's version, baked in a crust and served with a cream sauce:

Select several very large onions, wipe them without peeling and drop them into boiling water for several minutes. Remove and let cool. Cut off the top and carefully scoop out the interior with a knife, leaving the outer wall intact. Add 5–6 more peeled (raw) onions to the onion pulp removed from the interior. Cut up or finely chop all the onions together. Pour the chopped onions into a sauce pan, add ¾ glass cream, and boil until they are as soft as kasha. Rub through a sieve. Remove a fillet from a large young chicken, scrape it with a knife, and pound in a mortar. Add 4 eggs, ½ pound melted butter, 4 finely chopped sprats [a species of small herring], a little grated cheese, a French roll (without the crust) soaked in milk and squeezed out, and a little salt and pepper. Add the onion puree, mix everything, and fill the prepared onion shells.

After this, prepare short pastry, roll it out as thin as possible, and cut it into rectangles with a cutting wheel. Place a stuffed onion in the middle of each rectangle and fold up the four corners of dough. Pinch the leaves together tight in the middle and paint the sides with egg white using a feather. Let them dry slightly and bake in a saucepan or small basin with fat, Russian butter, or half fat and half Russian butter.

Serve at the table with the following cream sauce: Melt 1 spoon butter in a saucepan, mix with 1 spoon flour and dilute with ½ glass of cream. Add a little salt, pepper, and, if desired, the juice of ½ lemon. Boil thoroughly and serve in a sauceboat.

Some have said that an onion is not a vegetable that can stand alone, but these recipes for boiled, roasted, braised, and stuffed onions demonstrate that an onion can find its place as a show-piece on the menu.

8

Caramelized and Glazed

Onions are naturally sweet because they contain dextrose, a sugar 20 percent less sweet than sucrose. Sautéing while stirring slowly for a long time brings out the dextrose and "caramelizes" the onions. Recipe writers, especially the French, back in the days when recipes were truly written, tended to wax poetic about "the beautiful golden color" of caramelized onions. The key to achieving this is to stir gently but constantly. Sweet onions such as Walla Walla, Vidalia, or Maui are particularly good for caramelizing, because their high water content makes them very slow to brown.

In Morocco, caramelized onions are frequently served on couscous. In Ottoman Turkey, eggs were served poached on a bed of caramelized red onions.

Caramelized onions are used as a base for many dishes. Sometimes a small amount of sugar is added to onions, and while this may seem to caramelize in cooking, it is the sugar, not the onions, that is caramelizing and therefore onions that are prepared this way are known as glazed rather than caramelized. M. F. K. Fisher suggested that glazed onions were an ideal accompaniment for game.

Rufus Estes was born a slave in 1857. In 1911 he published *Good Things to Eat*, the first cookbook by an African American, in which he gives this recipe for glazed onions:

Peel the onions and place in a sauce pan with a little warmed fire and cook slowly till quite tender and the outside brown.

Rufus Estes.

Remove and serve on a dish. A little of the liquor, thickened with flour, may be served as a sauce.

Samuel Chamberlain was an American travel and food writer and illustrator. For many years, starting in the 1930s, first in France, then in New England, a French woman known simply as Clémentine was the cook for his family. Chamberlain, using the pseudonym Phineas Beck, wrote a book about her and her recipes, *Clémentine in the Kitchen*. This was Clémentine's recipe for glazed carrots and onions:

In a heavy saucepan brown 2 strips of lean bacon, diced in 1 tablespoon of butter. Remove the bacon scraps and in the fat remaining in the pan brown 12 tiny whole onions lightly on all sides. Then add six young carrots, cut into small pieces. Season the vegetables with a little salt, pepper and ½ teaspoon of sugar. When the carrots are lightly browned add ½ cup water. Simmer the vegetables covered, over a very low flame for about 10 minutes, or until they are tender and the liquid is reduced to a glaze. Remove the lid if necessary. Sprinkle with parsley before serving.

In Italy, *cipolline in agrodolce*, sweet-and-sour onions, is a well-known glazed onion dish. Here not only sugar but vinegar is added. This recipe is from Ada Boni (1881–1973), a Roman food writer whose books such as *Il talismano della felicità* ("The Talisman of Happiness," published in English as *The Talisman Italian Cook Book*) and *La cucina romana* ("Roman Cooking") remain among the most popular cookbooks in Italy. This recipe is from *La cucina romana*:

> For this dish use fairly small onions that are peeled and kept in cool water until they are ready to be cooked. Mince a little onion on the board with fat prosciutto, a pinch of garlic and a little parsley and put it in a pan with a little lard. Brown a little and then add a couple of spoonfuls of sugar. When the sugar is well melted, pour half a glass of vinegar in the pan. Season with salt and pepper and add a little broth or water so that the onions are almost submerged and can cook little by little. When fully cooked the onions will be well glazed, soaked in the thick sauce around them and with a shiny surface.

In Sicily, onions are sometimes glazed with orange blossom honey known as *zagara* from an Arabic word for white flowers. Arabic words are common on this once Arab-ruled island. This recipe for *cipuddini a carmela di zagara*, Sicilian for onions caramelized in zagara honey, is from Pino Correnti, a mid-twentieth-century writer from Catania who often wrote about things Sicilian. It also includes Marsala wine from the western side of the island.

> 2 kilos [4.4 pounds] white onions, 80 grams [about 3 ounces] pork lard, 300 grams [1 ½ cups] zagara honey, 1 glass dry Marsala wine, salt.
>
> Remove the onions' outer skin and boil them in lightly salted water, after having washed them. Drain and dry them

and fry in a pan of lard adding a half glass of dry Marsala and when it is nearly evaporated add the zagara honey, diluting it with a splash of Marsala if it is not fluid enough. Stir slowly with a wooden spoon until the honey has caramelized the onions, covering them with a soft sweet coating.

It is rare to find a vegetable side dish that is a greater treat than this. It is predictable that onion with pork fat, local honey, and Marsala wine would be wonderful, but caramelizing the onions adds a magical quality, a dimension of savoriness not unlike the Japanese concept of umami. Caramelized onions add this savoriness to any dish.

9

Creamed Onions

T hough fallen from grace, like many cream dishes, creamed onions were a great delicacy of the eighteenth, nineteenth, and early twentieth centuries, though the phrase "creamed onions" was rarely used before the twentieth century—instead, it was "onions in cream sauce." The dish's roots go even further back to white onion sauces and to stewed onion dishes, some of which were creamy.

Robert May, a Royalist chef during the tumultuous Civil War of seventeenth-century England, who cooked for the Royalists both when they were out of power and after the crown was restored, offered this sweet onion stew—a bit unusual because the onions were not just glazed with sugar but well buttered. His book was first published in 1665.

> Being peeled put them into boiling liquor and when they are boil'd, drain them in a cullender, and butter them whole with some boil'd currans, butter, sugar and beaten cinnamon.

But soon onion stews became mostly "creamed."

"Mrs. Child," Lydia Maria Francis Child, was one of the most extraordinary women of the nineteenth century. As the first American woman to write historical novels, she took on the rights of Native Americans. She not only was a leader in the movement to abolish slavery but was in the forefront of building the first American feminist movement. Her first novel, in 1824, *Hobomok*, was only signed "by an American." But by the time her cookbook came out, her name had become a national brand, clearly marked

Lydia Maria Child, 1865.

on the title page. One of the best-known writers in America, she eventually produced more than forty-seven books including novels, short stories, poetry, advice for homemakers, and political tracts. Her father was a baker who was credited with inventing crackers, or at least the name. She was always an innovator. *The American Frugal Housewife*, published in 1828, was one of the first cookbooks that ignored extravagant cuisine and presented an economic cooking style for those with limited income. It was a huge success and went through numerous editions and is still read in the twenty-first century. One recipe for boiled onions predates the term "creamed onions," but gives the idea:

> It is an excellent way of serving up onions, to chop them after they are boiled, and put them in a stewpan, with a little milk, butter, salt and pepper, and let them stew about fifteen minutes. This gives them a fine flavor, and they can be served very hot.

Pierre Blot, a Frenchman, in a very French intellectual way, became the leading chronicler of nineteenth-century American cuisine, paying careful attention to Native American and other roots of what was becoming a distinctly American style of food. He was the founder of the New York Cooking Academy and a "professor of gastronomy." Here is his recipe, keeping alive the Franglais tradition, for "Onions à la Crème" from his 1867 *Hand-Book of Practical Cookery, for Ladies and Professional Cooks*. His elegantly simple recipe remains one of the best for creamed onions:

> Only small white onions are prepared *à la crème*. Have water and a little salt on the fire, and drop two dozen small white

onions into it at the first boil. When cooked, drain and wipe them dry carefully, in order not to bruise them. Set a saucepan on the fire with about two ounces of butter in it, and when melted put the onions in, stirring gently for two or three minutes then turn about a gill of cream in, little by little, stirring the while, and as soon as the whole is in take from the fire, salt to taste, and serve hot.

In *The Cook Book by "Oscar" of the Waldorf,* Oscar Tschirky gives a recipe for "Boiled Onions with Cream," which comes from the béchamel onion sauce tradition:

Peel twelve medium sized onions, pare the roots without cutting them, place in a saucepan, cover with salted water, add a bunch of parsley, and boil for forty-five minutes. Take them from the saucepan, place them in a dish, cover with two gills of cream sauce, mixed with two tablespoonfuls of the broth the onions were cooked in, garnish and serve.

This was Tschirky's cream sauce recipe:

Put into a saucepan one ounce of flour and two ounces of butter, place it on a slow fire, and stir lightly with a spatula for two minutes, adding one wineglassful of Madeira, two ounces of caster ["superfine"] sugar and one teacupful of cream. Stir well again for two minutes, to avoid its coming to boil: take it from the fire, adding immediately one wineglassful of wine, stirring it lightly again.

Diat specified that creamed onions should be made with Bermuda onions and a mild sweet onion seems the right choice. But not everyone agrees. The earliest recipe I have found that was titled Creamed Onions was from *The Picayune's Creole Cook Book* originally published in 1901 by the New Orleans newspaper *The Times-Picayune*. In New Orleans fashion, they also called it *Oignons à la Crème*:

A dozen small white onions
A tablespoon of butter
A tablespoon of flour
½ pint of milk or cream
Salt and pepper to taste
Boil the onions as directed in the preceding recipe [that recipe has the onions put in cold water to peel then boiled with salt for about forty minutes]. When very tender take off the fire and drain. Pour over them the following cream sauce, which you will have prepared when almost ready to serve.

Put one tablespoon of flour into a sauce pan, and add a tablespoonful of butter. Set on the fire and let all blend together well, rubbing very smoothly without browning [this would work better if you first melted the butter, then added the flour and stirred]. Then add half a pint of milk. Stir continually till it boils. Season with salt and pepper to taste, and pour over the onions, and serve hot.

Rufus Estes gives this creamed onion recipe in his cookbook *Good Things to Eat*. In the nineteenth and early twentieth centuries this was an extremely popular American dish.

Peel twelve medium sized onions, pare the roots without cutting them, place in a sauce pan, cover with salted water, add a bunch of parsley, and boil for forty-five minutes: take them from the saucepan, place them on a dish, covering with two gills of cream sauce, mixed with two tablespoons of broth, garnish and serve.

.   .   .

Perhaps the greatest tribute to creamed onions is the 1941 Warner Brothers film *They Died with Their Boots On*, with Errol Flynn's portrayal of U.S. Calvary disaster George Armstrong Custer. The title may be the film's only historically accurate statement. Those who watch the film will learn little about the survival struggle of the Sioux and the campaign to destroy them, but they will learn a lot about onions. Probably because the film is mostly based on the account of his widow, Elizabeth Custer, her husband is given a heroic image not matched by the historic record, but the screenwriters also clearly took to heart her descriptions of her husband's love of onions. This is almost a movie about onions.

Early in the story we see the brash West Point cadet devouring onions like apples. Onions continue in the movie with more walk-ons than his cavalry. Custer is in a bar munching on scallions, waving the greens to the beat when he first hears the Irish song "Garyowen" (which the film erroneously portrays as an English song).

He eats a few green onions before his big courtship scene with Olivia de Havilland. She complains of onion breath and he says in a wounded tone, "Don't you like onions?"

And so in their big love scene they munch on green onions, Olivia's eyes already watering from them, when Custer selects one out for her. "See that fine long grain," he says. "That will have a bite to it," and he hands it to her.

The biggest onion scene occurs when he is a young cavalry lieutenant in the Civil War. He steps into a Washington, D.C., restaurant and orders the last serving of creamed onions. These creamed onions are made with Bermuda onions, exactly as Diat recommended.

Huge and round Sydney Greenstreet shows up in the restaurant as General Winfield Scott. The always ambitious Custer advances his career by sharing his creamed onions with the general.

As the general and the young lieutenant leave the restaurant, they are still talking onions. "It's a fatal mistake to steam onions," opines the general.

"Even when they are sealed in a container?" asks the junior officer.

"Under any circumstances," says the general. "You steam all the best out of them."

The lieutenant then quips, "General, you certainly know your onions," which would have been an anachronism for the 1860s, especially if the expression truly came from C. T. Onions, the editor, who wasn't even born until 1873.

Today, creamed onions are hard to find unless you make them yourself, which you should. With cream sauces out of favor, creamed onions stand as an abandoned artifact from the days when we were allowed to be fat and happy.

10

Fried

F ried onions go back almost to the beginning of cooking onions at all, and their popularity spans the globe. A book from the first century c.e. attributed to Apicius indicated that fried bulbs should be served with wine sauce. And while Americans may think of fried onion rings as something typically American, they are a favored garnish in Central Europe, especially Germany, and in Southeast Asia, where they are sometime served with fried rice.

India has many fried onion dishes—a number of types of rings and several fritters. *Bhone piaz ke lache* are fried onions, not in rings but shredded and crisped. This dish dates from the Muslim Moghul Empire, a dynasty that was originally Mongol and ruled a part of India from the sixteenth to the nineteenth centuries, contributing many ideas to Indian cooking. *Bhone piaz ke lache* usually accompany meat and rice dishes, adding a little crunch. This advice on making the dish is from Julie Sahni's 1980 book, *Classic Indian Cooking*:

> First, slice the onions in thin shreds . . . Heat vegetable oil in a *kadhai* or frying pan over medium high heat until very hot but not smoking (375–400 degrees F). Add the onion slices and fry, stirring constantly, until they turn dark brown. (Watch carefully that they do not blacken or burn, which will make them taste bitter.) The time will depend on the quantity of onions being fried. Two cups of thinly sliced onions will take about 25 to 30 minutes.
>
> It is best to serve fried onions immediately after removing from skillet and draining on paper towels. This is when they are at their crispest. If they need to sit awhile, cover them well so that they do not soften.

Pushpesh Pant, one of India's most prolific food writers, has a recipe for onion bhajiya, onion rings from southern India scented with ajwain, a strongly perfumed tiny fruit that looks like cumin but tastes more like thyme. Because the rings are fried by the spoonful rather than individually, these are more like fritters than what we think of as fried onion rings.

1 cup chickpea flour
½ teaspoon baking soda

2 teaspoons ajwain seeds
6 large onions cut into thin rings
vegetable oil for deep-frying
salt

Put the chickpea flour in a large bowl and stir in enough water to make a thick batter. Add the baking soda and ajwain seeds and season with salt. Add the onion rings and mix well to coat the onions with the batter.

Heat enough oil for deep-frying in a kadhai or deep, heavy-based pan to 350 degrees F or until a cube of bread browns in 30 seconds. Using a ladle, very carefully drop spoonfuls of coated onions into the hot oil and deep-fry for about 3–4 minutes or until golden brown. Remove with a slotted spoon and drain on a paper towel. Keep the fritter warm while making the others in the same way.

Another onion fritter from southern India, *pakora*, made with chopped onions, has become a standard appetizer at Indian restaurants. This is also Pant's recipe:

1 cup chickpea flour
2 tablespoons rice flour
¾ cup vegetable oil
3 medium sized onions finely chopped
1 ½ teaspoons chili powder
2 tablespoons finely chopped coriander (cilantro leaves)
salt
vegetable oil for deep-frying

Combine the flours, oil, onions, chili powder and coriander together in a bowl. Season with salt and mix in 1 teaspoon of water to make a stiff batter.

Heat enough oil for deep-frying in a kadhai or deep, heavy-based pan to 350 degrees F or until a cube of bread browns in 30 seconds, then reduce the heat slightly. Working in batches, drop spoonfuls of the batter into the hot oil and deep-fry, turning frequently for about 2–3 minutes or until golden and crisp. Remove the pakoras with a slotted spoon and drain on a paper towel.

. . .

In Victorian England, Agnes Bertha Marshall recommended frying small onions, which are a great nuisance to peel. My recommendation, not hers, is to blanch them for a few seconds in boiling water before peeling. Made with whole buttons rather than rings, this is one of the more complicated and delectable variations on fried onions:

Put some small white onions that have been peeled into a stew pan with cold water and a little salt, and bring them to the boil; then strain and put them into a clean stewpan to cook for one hour with two ounces of butter [for one quart of onions], a dust of coralline pepper [pink peppercorns], the juice of a lemon, and a quarter of a pint of white stock, cover the pan over and let them cook steadily on the side of the stove; take up when tender, and roll them in finely chopped parsley. And then into fine flour and whole beaten up eggs and place them in a frying basket, and fry them in a clean boiling fat till a pretty golden colour; dish up on a bed of crisply fried parsley, and serve at once, with the following sauce in a boat: Take the liquor in which the onions were cooked, and mix it with a gill of reduced Veloute sauce [a stock thickened by butter and flour; hers adds lemon juice and cream], boil up, tammy [a cloth through which sauces are pressed) and use.

These are very good to serve as a garnish with rumpsteak or roast mutton.

Escoffier, in keeping with his claim of being a simplifier, offered a very modest recipe for fried onion rings, and in fact Escoffier was never more simple:

Cut into rings a half centimeter [a little less than a quarter inch] thick, season with salt and pepper, cover with flour and fry in hot oil.

In America at the time of the Civil War, the most common way to serve onions was fried, and the dish has remained popular. American food writer John Mariani, in his 1983 *Dictionary of American Food & Drink*, gave the standard fried onion ring recipe but with the charming twist of using cornmeal:

Slice a large onion into rings, soak in a mixture of 1 beaten egg and ⅓ cup of milk. Dip into flour mixed with cornmeal, then into bread crumbs. Fry in hot oil till golden brown.

Another variation is offered by Evelyn Rogers of Vidalia, Georgia, in her book *Sweet Vidalia Onions* (1986). In this recipe, called French Fried Onion Rings, the onions are fried in beer batter. The use of buckwheat, a common short-term summer crop in Georgia, is a nice local touch.

1 cup buckwheat flour or all-purpose flour
1 cup beer
2 jumbo Vidalia onions
2 tablespoons corn meal
¾ tablespoon salt
4 cups oil
Combine flour, meal, beer and salt in mixing bowl stirring fast and thoroughly. Let sit about 3 hours at room temperature. Peel, wash, and slice onions, separate into rings and soak in ice water for 30 minutes. Towel dry. Heat oil in deep fry pot. Dip each ring separately into batter. Drop into hot oil. Fry in oil until brown. Onion rings may be placed in baking dish and kept in oven at 200 degrees F until ready to serve.

On Maui, fried sweet Kula onions are simple to make. The onions are sliced and tossed in flour and then fried in hot vegetable oil. This, like Escoffier's recipe, gets right to the point. Fried onions rings, just floured or batter-dipped and fried, in very hot oil, are an indulgence to be cherished, and if we disparage fried food, we will miss this one.

11

Eggs and Onions

All omelette-eating cultures, which is a considerable list, know onion omelettes. Cora Millet-Robinet included a recipe for one in her 1844 book, *Maison rustique des dames*, but first she devoted a page to the subject of making omelettes. She begins:

> Although everyone knows how to make an omelet, they are often badly made. I would go so far as to say that very few cooks know how to make them properly.

I was pleased to read this because I very much believe it. It is why I avoid ordering omelettes in restaurants. But then she goes on to suggest things with which I disagree. She suggests beating some milk into the eggs, which I count as a travesty. She also suggests using beer. But she does hit on the heart of the matter when she writes, "It should be moist, that is to say that it should weep round the edges where the heat has not caused it to entirely solidify."

Here is her recipe for an onion omelette, which she advises is a lunchtime dish. In fairness, she adds the milk to the onions, not the eggs, so this may be forgivable:

Slice some onions and cook them in a covered saucepan with some butter, salt, and pepper. Add a little milk and let it reduce, stirring frequently. Mix this purée with the eggs to make the omelet. You can also brown the onions in butter before adding the eggs to them.

There are interesting variations on onions and scrambled eggs. Here is the 1913 recipe of Spanish author Emilia Pardo Bazán:

Beat a half dozen eggs and put them in a casserole. Season with salt and pepper. Put a casserole on a low fire with a piece of pork fat stirring with a wooden spoon until it begins to thicken. Then add three or four spoonfuls of minced onion already softened in a skillet. After a few seconds put in a dish and serve with toast.

Kitâb Wasf al-Atima al-Mutada, the fourteenth-century collection of thirteenth-century Arab recipes, offers this recipe for *Muba'tharat al-basal*, onion scramble:

Cut up onions well, then strain away their juice, then throw them in the tajine and pour over them a sufficiency of fresh sesame oil, then fry them in that sesame oil. Then pour eggs upon them, after beating them well until the yolks are mixed with the whites. Put a little salt and spices with them and do not stop observing the fire and stirring until it is pleasing.

In the nineteenth century, Pellegrino Artusi, a wealthy silk merchant in Florence, collected his favorite Tuscan recipes and in 1891, failing to find a publisher, self-published them. His *La scienza in cucina e l'arte di mangiar bene*, "The Science of Cooking and the Art of Eating Well," has been sold in the food section of almost every bookstore in Italy ever since. This is his recipe for "onion frittata," an Italian classic:

Use large white onions [the strong-tasting summer onions in Italy]. Cut them into slices half a finger thick and soak them for at least an hour in cool water. Drain them well and sauté them in lard or oil; when they begin to brown, salt them well, and stir the eggs into the pan. When the frittata begins to firm up flip it with the aid of a plate and cook the other side, being careful not to let it burn. [Artusi does not say how many eggs. If it is one to two onions use six eggs.]

Eggs cooked with onions are not always scrambled. In Turkey the eggs are poached to make *soğanlı yumurta*, caramelized onions and eggs. The dish appears to have some religious significance in Turkey. The sultans of the Ottoman Empire, who ruled Turkey for more than seven centuries, resided in the Topkapı

Palace in Istanbul for more than four hundred years but left for the Muslim holiday of Ramadan to pay homage to a cloak supposedly worn by the prophet Muhammad. On the fifteenth day of the holiday, they returned to the palace and ate soğanlı yumurta. Making this simple dish well was the path to promotion in the royal pantry. This is not unreasonable. Both eggs and caramelized onions demand perfect handling. If I had cooks, I would only hire ones who could make perfect poached eggs, though perfectly caramelized onions would be an equally valid test. This recipe is from professor of Turkish and culinary expert Ayla Algar:

> Quarter 2 large red onions and slice paper-thin. Heat 4 tablespoons unsalted butter in a heavy skillet and add onions. Sprinkle with salt and cook over very low heat, stirring occasionally, for at least 40 to 50 minutes, until onions turn reddish-brown and become slightly crisp. Take care not to burn them. As onions cook and become dry, sprinkle in some water. When onions are caramelized sprinkle with vinegar, ground allspice, ground cinnamon, freshly ground black pepper and 1 ½ teaspoons of sugar and mix thoroughly.
>
> Make three or four depressions in the onions and break an egg into each. Sprinkle with a little salt and pepper, cover, and cook gently until eggs are covered with a transparent film. Serve immediately.
>
> [The trick here, if you ever want to make it in the sultan's kitchen, is that the eggs must be cooked but the yolk remains liquid.]

In my kitchen, no doubt a step down from the sultan's, there is only one way to make an omelette. Caramelize onions. Then beat three eggs with a fork (always make one omelette at a time) and pour the beaten eggs into a skillet with ample melted salted butter on a medium heat. Stir the eggs rapidly with a fork and as soon as they start to solidify, remove from the heat, add the onions, fold, and slide onto a plate. There should be no browning of the egg. This takes a little dexterity, but only the nimble can make a good omelette, which is why I think it is the best test of a cook's skill.

12

Puddings, Custards, and Cakes

Historically, desserts were an afterthought in European cuisine. Until the sixteenth century, sugar was not commonplace in Europe and there were few sweeteners—mostly honey. Sweetness was so rare that parsnips were valued for their ability to lend sweetness to a dish. Even into the nineteenth century, puddings, custards, and cakes were often savory. A dessert was denoted as an exception, as in "dessert pudding" or "dessert custard." The savory versions often involved onions.

Puddings, both savory and sweet, used to be a mainstay of British cooking. Onion pudding was a staple of farmers in

England during the winter months because onions stored so well. Mrs. Beeton, chronicler of the standards rather than innovator, gave this recipe:

> Ingredients: 8 ounces of flour. 2 ounces of breadcrumbs. 3 or 4 ounces of butter. (1 spoonful of olive oil may be substituted.) 1 teaspoonful of baking powder. 1 spoonful of saltwater. For the Mixture: 3 or 4 large mild onions, 2 tablespoonsful of breadcrumbs, ¼ teaspoonful of sage, salt and pepper, 1 or 2 ounces of butter.
>
> Method: Cut the peeled onions into small dice, place them in a pie dish, with the breadcrumbs, butter and sage, and season with salt and pepper, cover closely and bake gently for 1 hour. Rub the butter into the flour and breadcrumbs, add the baking powder and salt, and sufficient water to form a rather stiff paste. Line a basin with the paste, put in the [onion] mixture when cool, cover with paste and afterwards with 2 or 3 folds of greased paper and steam for 2 hours. Serve in the basin and send brown sauce to table separately.

In the mid-nineteenth century, onion custard was popular in America. *Godey's Lady's Book* offered this recipe in 1860:

> Peel and slice some mild onions (ten or twelve proportion to their size) and fry them in fresh butter, draining them well when you take them up; then mince them as fine as possible; beat four eggs very light and stir them very gradually into a pint of milk, in turn with the minced onions; season the whole with plenty of ground nutmeg, and stir it very hard; then put

it into a deep white dish, and bake it about a quarter of an hour. Send it to the table as a side dish, to be eaten with meat or poultry. It is a French preparation of onions and will be found very fine.

Jane Grigson wrote this recipe for *teisen nionod*, Welsh onion cake:

2 pounds firm potatoes, preferably *Desirée* or waxy new potatoes
1 pound onions
4–5 ounces butter
pepper and salt
Peel or scrape the potatoes, then slice them paper thin, on a mandolin or the cucumber blade of a grater, into a bowl of cold water. Swish them about well to get rid of the starchy juice, then dry them in a clean tea towel. Peel and slice the onions.

Take a shallow dish or oblong cake tin and grease it with a butter paper (if you intend to turn the cake out at the end, it is a good idea to line the dish or tin with Bakewell paper or foil before greasing it). Put in a layer of potatoes, then a layer of onions and so on, finishing with potatoes. Season the layers and dot them with butter, leaving about 1 ounce to melt and pour over the top layer. Cover the dish with foil— don't worry if the vegetables mount up above the dish, they subside as they cook. Bake at 350 degrees for 1 ½ hours removing the foil for the last half hour so the top can brown.

When the vegetables are cooked but not too soft, put a serving dish on top of the tin and reverse it quickly. Ease the paper or foil and remove the tin. Flash under the grill for a few minutes to brown the top. There is, on the other hand, no reason why you shouldn't serve the onion cake in its cooking dish like a French gratin. If you decide on this kind of treatment there is no reason to line the tin with paper or foil.

This is a good example of why a cake does not have to be a dessert.

13

Tarts and Pies

P ies, too, were savory before they were sweet. William Ellis's writings on farming were so popular in the early eighteenth century that people went to see his farm in Hertfordshire, England, from all over Europe. He gave this recipe for onion pies:

ONION PYE made by laboring Men's Wives—
They mix chopt apples and onions in equal quantities, and with some sugar put them into dough-crust and bake them: This by some is thought to make as good a pie as pumkins do. It is Hertfordshire contrivance.

But for most, Hertfordshire aside, an onion pie is a savory dish. Hannah Glasse, a contemporary of Ellis, gave this recipe for onion pie. It has much in common with the Hertfordshire version but is savory and more elaborate and was published three years earlier than Ellis's:

> Wash and pare some Potatoes, and cut them in Slices, peel some Onions, cut them in Slices, pare some Apples and slice them, make a good Crust, cover your Dish, lay a quarter of a pound of Butter all over, take a quarter of an Ounce of Mace beat fine, a Nutmeg grated, a tea spoon of beaten Pepper, three tea spoonfuls of Salt, mix all together strew some over the Butter, lay a Layer of Potatoes, a Layer of Onions, a Layer of Apples, a Layer of Eggs [probably hardboiled and sliced], and so on, til you have filled your Pye, strewing a little of the Seasoning between each Layer, and a quarter Pound of Butter in Bits, and Six Spoonsful of water. Close your Pye and bake it an Hour and a half: A Pound of Potatoes, a Pound of Onion, a Pound of Apples, and twelve Eggs will do.

Onion pies appeared over the centuries in many places— across Europe and all the way to Cajun Louisiana. In Louisiana, where it is called an "onion cake," it is baked in a crust like a pie. The filling, according to Louisiana chef John D. Folse, includes onions (he uses Vidalia), cream cheese, bacon, chives, caraway seeds, and eggs.

This one, from Italy, is for boiled onion pie, *Cipolle lessate in torta*, from Ada Boni's recipe in her 1929 *Il talismano della felicità*:

Clean the onions, cutting off the roots and the upper part and peel off the outer skin. Cut them into thin slices, dip them in boiling water, lightly salted and leave them cooking until they are limp. Put them in a casserole with 50 grams of butter [about two ounces]. Season them with salt, pepper and nutmeg and cook them over a very moderate heat until they fall apart but do not let them brown.

With a somewhat less fat puff pastry made with 100 grams [3 ½ ounces] of butter and 150 grams [5 ⅓ ounces] of flour, spread the pastry in a 20-centimeter-diameter [8-inch] spring form and put it on a baking sheet. Trim off the excess dough and puncture the bottom of the dough with a fork.

Put an egg and a spoonful of flour in a bowl and add grated gruyere cheese. Dissolve in milk or, even better, with cream, and when the onions have cooled, combine with this mixture. Pour it into the pasta and fill it. Place it in a moderate oven for about an hour until the dough is dark and crunchy.

Take it out of the oven, remove the side ring and slide onto a plate. Serve hot.

The Russians have a tradition of onion-stuffed pastry. Piroshki are small pastries stuffed with meat and onion, or hard-boiled eggs and onions, or onions and cabbage. They are usually served with soup. A pirog is a larger pastry made with the same ingredients. Often in Russia, rather than celebrating a birthday, the saint's day of the saint after which someone is named is celebrated. Pirogi are often served for this occasion. This recipe for a name-day pirogue comes from Wanda L. Frolov's 1947 book about her Russian cook, *Katish: Our Russian Cook*:

Line a square tin, about 1 ½ inches deep, with your chosen pastry [this might be puff pastry or a yeast dough]. Cover the bottom with a layer of cold boiled rice. Over this sprinkle a layer of lightly browned green onions. Then put in a layer of chopped hard-boiled egg. Next a somewhat thicker layer of any good white fish which has been gently poached in a little water seasoned with bay leaf, a slice of onion, salt and some peppercorns. The fish should be moist and broken into small chunks but not flaked. On top of the fish put some onions, then a layer of chopped eggs, then more rice. Repeat this until the pan is full, seeing that each layer is properly seasoned with salt and pepper. Sprinkle a little of the fish boullion on top of the filling and dot with butter. Then seal on the top crust and pierce with a fork. Bake in hot oven 425 degrees F, until the crust is cooked and brown.

Another, simpler Russian onion tartlet recipe, for *Vatrushki s lukom* ("buns with onions"), comes from Elena Molokhovets's nineteenth-century cookbook:

Prepare yeast dough or short pastry. Cut the dough into pieces, roll out the flat cakes, cover with finely shredded onions fried in nut oil with salt and a little pepper. Turn up and pinch the edges all around. Set aside to rise, paint with olive oil. And bake in the oven. To serve, brush on more olive oil or nut oil.

This Russian tartlet is similar to the *pituni*, Sicilian fried onion turnover, described by Mary Taylor Simeti in her 1989 book on

Sicilian food, *Pomp and Sustenance.* These little half-moon fried pastries are filled with finely sliced onions sautéed in olive oil with capers.

Variations of savory onion tarts are local specialties of many French regions. Louis Diat, originally from the Auvergne in central France, served little onion tartlets as side dishes in his New York restaurant. This was his 1941 recipe:

> Line 24 very small tartlets molds with pie crust paste [dough made with flour, butter, lard, salt, and water]. Chop three onions and brown in butter. Put in the tartlets. Make a custard of 2 well-beaten eggs and 1 cup of milk. Add salt, a pinch of paprika, and a pinch of nutmeg. Pour over the onions and bake in a hot oven for ten to fifteen minutes.

In Picardie and other regions of northern France there is *flamiche* or *flamique*, a tart of onions or sometimes leeks. Since the name means "Flemish," it probably originated in Flanders.

Alsatians make *zeweewai* or *flan aux oignons.* Pierre Gaertner, former chef of celebrated Alsatian restaurant Aux Armes de France, near Colmar in Ammerschwihr, and a student of Ferdinand Point, one of the greats of modern French cooking, gave this recipe for his Alsatian onion tart:

> 350 gram [¾ pound] short dough [1 cup flour, big pinch of salt, 9 ounces butter, ⅓ cup water, 1 egg yolk worked in a mixing bowl in this order]
> 600 grams [1⅓ pounds] onions
> 150 grams [5 ounces] butter

1 tablespoon oil

4 eggs

¼ liter [1 cup] crème fraîche

¼ liter [1 cup] milk

1 tablespoon flour

1 pinch salt

1 full turn of black pepper mill

a touch of nutmeg

Peel and chop the onions. Sauté in oil and butter until it turns color—about 20 minutes. Add flour and mix well and let it cook a few moments more. Off of the burner add the crème and the milk. After a few seconds add the eggs, well-beaten. Season with salt, pepper and nutmeg.

Place the dough in a buttered tart mold, fill it with the mixture, and bake in a moderate oven (350 degrees F).

Remove from the tart mold and serve hot.

Good chefs never tell you everything, but if you saw his onion tart you would observe that he sliced onion rings and, before baking, arranged them around the tart, larger ones on the outside and smaller ones toward the center—a nice presentation. He liked to serve the tart with the local Côte d'Ammerschwihr Riesling—dry, crisp, and fruity—and if you can find a good Alsatian Riesling—not that hard to find—you will be happy.

Various onion tarts appear throughout France until Nice, where the influence clearly comes from nearby Italy. The *pissaladiéra* appears to be a Niçoise pizza, consisting of pizza dough topped with onions, anchovies, and Niçoise olives. Today, in borderless Europe, some chefs in Nice succumb to the popularity of actual pizza and add tomato sauce, but that is not an authentic pissaladiéra. In some preparations, it looks like a bread, a focaccia with a light dusting of onions, but this too is incorrect. To be a pissaladiéra, it should have a thick bed of them, thus making it a tart.

The flamboyant mayor of Nice, Jacques Médecin, before he was jailed in the early 1990s for corruption, handed me, and most everyone he met, his impassioned book of Niçoise recipes. He loved Nice, where his father had been mayor before him, and though Médicin's financial practices were highly questionable, he was incorruptible when it came to matters of Niçoise gastronomy. He pointed out that the name *pissaladiéra* had nothing to do with pizza, and that the name stemmed instead from the original practice of brushing the dough with a string that had been dipped in *pissala*, a traditional puree made from salted fish. The mayor gave a recipe for salting anchovies over weeks to make this puree, but also suggested the quick way: buy salt-cured anchovies and soak them for twelve hours in cool running water. Then force the fish through a sieve.

He warned against fraud—that there were many fraudulent versions of this dish—and that a real pissaladiéra had onions piled on top in the same thickness as the crust. Here is his recipe:

For ten servings
500 grams of bread dough [or pizza dough]
3 Kilos [6.6 pounds] of onions
2 cloves of garlic
50 grams of black Nice olives
ten anchovy filets

four tablespoons of pissala

bouquet garni

olive oil

salt and pepper

1. Finely mince 3 kilos of onions, lightly salt them, and let them cook lightly under a low heat in a covered casserole, with 2 crushed garlic cloves and a small bouquet garni and a tablespoon of olive oil. The onions should become quite cooked without having taken on any color.

2. Take the bread dough from a baker and put in a pan 1.5 centimeters thick in a round with a 25-centimeter circumference. [You are not supposed to say this, but a pizza pan would work well for this.]

3. Let it rise in a warm place and when the volume of the dough has doubled heat it in the oven for ten minutes.

4. Remove the bouquet garni from the onions and spread them thickly on the dough. Level it with a wooden spoon, arrange the olives like the spokes on a bicycle and then the anchovy filets. Spread the pissala over all of the surface. Drizzle with olive oil.

5. Put in a hot oven for fifteen minutes.

· · ·

Back in the United States, in Georgia, they so believe in the sweetness of Vidalia onions that, as in old-time Hertfordshire, they bake them in pies and cakes for dessert. This happens in sweet onion regions. One year at the Walla Walla Onion Festival the prize-winning recipe was for Marguerite Daltoso's German chocolate onion cake with Walla Walla onions. In Georgia, Gail

Barker won first place in the 1987 Vidalia Onion Cook-off for her Lemon Onion Pie:

3 cups boiled sweet Vidalia Onions

2 cups sugar

2 tablespoons butter or margarine, melted

3 eggs, beaten

2 tablespoons flour

3 tablespoons lemon extract

2 unbaked pie crusts

1 small container whipped topping

Place drained boiled onions in blender and puree until smooth. Add sugar and butter. Mix well. Add eggs, flour, and lemon extract and mix well. Pierce bottom of unbaked pie crust with fork. Add 2 ¼ cups of filling to each crust. Bake at 350 degrees F until crusts are brown. Cool and top with cool whip. Garnish with lemon twists.

She then adds that you can replace the lemon extract with 3 tablespoons coconut extract and garnish with grated coconut and have a "coconut onion pie."

For most of us, though, onions remain in the realm of the savory—likely a wise choice.

14

Bloody Onions

B lood and alliums is an ancient combination. One of the
Sumerian tablets from 1730 B.C.E. gives a recipe for *zukanda*,
a meatless soup from water, fat, kurrat (leek), cilantro, and garlic,
all thickened with blood and sour milk. Eating blood is forbidden
in both Islamic and Jewish law and so this dish has not survived
in Iraq.

Eating blood is controversial in the Catholic Church as well,
forbidden on holy days. The metaphor of eating blood plays a role
in European literature. In Émile Zola's novel set in the nineteenth-
century Les Halles market, *Le ventre de Paris* (*The Belly of
Paris*), Florent, with a little girl on his lap, tells horrifying stories

of his experiences in the penal colony as the family gathers around the kitchen, preparing the blood for the sausage known as boudin noir. In Camilo José Cela's novel of the Spanish Civil War in his native Galicia, *Mazurca para dos raiche* (*Mazurka for Two Dead Men*), Benicia, whom half the town desires and who is said to have lovely breasts, makes blood sausages for all the village to watch, while topless.

Blood is a source of nutrition, considered by many a valuable by-product of the slaughtering of animals. Blood dishes usually involve onions. This is not unique to European cooking. In China, in Fujian on the southeastern coast, pigs' blood is coagulated and cut into squares that are stir-fried like bean curd along with green Welsh onions.

In a number of European languages, "blood and onions" is a common phrase—*sang amb ceba* in Catalan, *sangre encebollada* in Andalusian, or *hagymás vér* in Hungarian.

In Budapest, it is common to slaughter a chicken over a skillet, sautéing the blood with onions. Country people have access to a greater variety of blood including duck, goose, and pig. Budapest food writer Ilona Horváth in a 1993 cookbook gave this recipe:

Duck's or goose's blood or ½ liter pig's blood, 3 tablespoons oil or 4 dkg lard, 1onion, paprika or black pepper, salt.

Slice the onions thin and wilt them in hot oil, we add to it thinly sliced or cubed clotted blood. Salt it and add spices and fry it stirring for 6–8 minutes.

Serve it with potatoes and pickles or other sour stuff.

Another recipe from the same book is for blood sausages. Several bread rolls are cut into cubes, toasted, and then soaked in milk. This is cooked with rice, ground meat, and bacon and then enough blood is added for a soup-like consistency. It is then mixed with sautéed onions and marjoram and stuffed in a large intestine casing. The sausage is then roasted and served with "a vinegary horseradish."

.   .   .

Rice is more typical than onion as filler for blood sausage. In Spain it is always done with rice, but in Basque Country, where each province has its own cuisine, Guipúzcoa and Vizcaya reject rice and make their blood sausage with onions. José Maria Busca Isusi, the renowned twentieth-century Basque food writer, as loyal to his native Guipúzcoa as he is to his Basqueness, defended their blood sausage: "Onions and leeks have distinctive and unadulterated flavors and are widely used as spices in cooking, whereas rice, with its almost imperceptible taste, can add nothing more to sausage than its physical characteristics."

There are many Basque onion traditions such as the Vizcaina sauce used on salt cod, which is made from onions and choricero peppers and sweet green onions that grow along the Bidasoa river, a gentle river that forms part of the French border. These green onions are only used in the French Basque provinces. But on the Spanish side, in the provinces of Guipúzcoa and Vizcaya, one of the important uses of onions is in blood sausages known in Basque as *odolkiak*. Sometimes, especially in the ruggedly stunning highlands of central Vizcaya, they are made not with pig's blood but with blood and fat from lambs, and are called *buskantzak*. It is difficult to make *buskantzak* unless you live in a sheep region or have ranchers for friends. (I do.) Busca Isusi offered this recipe and specifies that the best results come from using a young, well-fattened, castrated male lamb. It can be seen that he was not a Mrs. Beeton or Fannie Farmer trying to make recipes accessible to simple households. Instead, a typical Basque, he was concerned with the accurate preservation of culture and tradition.

In this recipe he also demonstrates his claim that the secret to a good blood sausage is the proper cooking of the onions:

13 pounds onions, not sweet

18 large leeks, white part only

4 ½ pounds fat from the kidney and peritoneum [caul fat] or
    lard

2 ½ quarts uncoagulated blood

6 choricero red peppers very finely chopped

1 ounce dried ground clove

1 ounce ground anise

3 ounces ground black pepper

3 ounces powdered oregano

3 ounces ground cinnamon

salt to taste

Chop the onions and leeks very finely and cook slowly for about ten hours in lard or a little fat from the animal. As the mixture is heating, the onions and leeks will release the natural vegetable juices in which they will continue cooking. If the temperature is raised significantly, the abundant sugars in the onion can caramelize and even burn, something which should be avoided at all costs. After this cooking, the mixture should be like a thick puree of a creamy brown color.

Chop the remaining fat very finely and place in a separate container. Mix in the blood completely integrating the two ingredients then mix in the puree of onions and leeks. It is advantageous to combine these mixtures in a clay receptacle surrounded by lukewarm water. Otherwise the fat remains hardened and mixes badly.

Add the chopped peppers and spices and mix again to distribute uniformly. Stuffed the mixture into cleaned intestines and stomach (or sausage casings) and scald until the mixture is well coagulated.

The blood sausage never uses the green of the leeks. This part is saved and put in a broth in which the sausages are boiled. The leeks act as a cushion to keep the delicate sausages from breaking until they are done. Then the leek broth is eaten as a soup.

Busca Isusi also gave a recipe for *frikatza*, a traditional dish of lamb intestines, blood, onions, and eggs:

The intestines of the suckling lamb are not strong enough for stuffing. The lamb's blood is collected upon butchering of the animal and coagulating in a mold for cooking. The intestines are cooked and cut up. The blood also cut up is fried with onion and the intestines. It is then added to beaten eggs.

In Valencia, a Catalan-speaking region on the other side of Spain, blood is also coagulated, then cut up and fried with pine nuts and onions to make *sang amb ceba*.

.   .   .

Civet, a medieval dish whose name means "onion," is a game stew that starts with onions and ends with blood. It is possible that the original onion and game stew did not include blood, but when you kill game you have its blood, a nutritious and valuable food, and it didn't take long to realize that finishing the stew by stirring in the blood at a low temperature created a thick, dark sauce.

Originally a civet was made with hare. For centuries civet recipes called for hare before deer, wild boar, and other wild red meat started being used. The Basques make civet with rabbit rather than hare, and while the ears are similar, the difference in the meat is like that between chicken and venison.

Personally, I like best *civet de sanglier*, wild boar, and when I lived in Paris I used to wait for these hairy hulks to be hung outside the butchers. The butcher would also supply the blood, and if he was out of boar blood, he would sell domestic pig blood, which also works quite well. Civet always starts by stewing the game with onions. I used about a dozen little pearl onions. I would first sauté the game in sliced onions and dices of *poitrine fumée*. This is cured pork chest smoked in beech, which, though commonly available anywhere in France, can be hard to come by elsewhere, and, along with wild boar itself, and with debating subjects that don't matter, is what I miss most about France.

After the game is browned on all sides, it is flamed in an ample shot of brandy. I always stew the game and onions with some bay leaves, salt, and a few peppercorns in red wine, very slowly for a few hours. Since game season is fall, which is also chestnut time, I add some husked chestnuts. It is also the season for wild mushrooms. *Trompette de la mort* is not only a wonderfully descriptive name for these little black horns but in addition to their woodland flavor, the mushrooms are one of the few truly black foods and something that will actually be darker than a sauce of cooked blood. They contrast well with white pearl onions. When the meat is tender, add some crème fraîche at a high temperature so that it reduces very quickly, and then under low heat slowly add the blood until it creates a thick, dark sauce.

This civet recipe is my own. While I don't think of myself as a historic food figure, I put this recipe together by studying old French recipes. In the ten years I lived in Paris I delighted French friends and visitors every fall with this civet dish made with boar or deer. If you can get the ingredients, it is a luxurious pleasure on a cold autumn night.

An early version, from fifteenth-century England, written in Middle English, was called *hare yn cyve*, hare civet, or hare in onion. This medieval dish did not call for any blood, but, typical of the period, included a great deal of spices such as mace, cloves, and ginger, and was also cooked in wine. If blood was added it was not called a civet, despite the presence of onions, but *hare yn talbut*. "Talbut" in Middle English was a hunting dog.

The earliest French civets, and *civet* is a French word, were thickened with breadcrumbs rather than blood, and they had many other things in them, such as oysters. But they always had their namesake, onions. And by the seventeenth century, at least in France, the hare and onion stew known as civet was finished with blood.

These bloody onion dishes may sound horrifying, but actually, they are all exquisite treats, at least to me.

15

A Pickle

It may be surprising that onions, which keep extremely well if stored properly, would be such a popular candidate for pickling, which is generally for preserving things that otherwise would spoil. Pickling onions has been popular, though, for thousands of years, and the only explanation is that pickled onions have a pleasant taste, with the fierceness of the raw flavor tamed and the natural sweetness blending well with the strong sourness of the pickle. Before the twentieth century, pickling was a way of keeping vegetables on hand throughout the winter months. Today, there is no real need for pickling, but certain vegetables such as onions, cucumbers, and green tomatoes continue to be pickled just because people enjoy them.

The recipe has never been stated more succinctly than in the fourteenth-century Arab text *Kitâb Wasf al-Atima al-Mutada*:

They are steeped in water and salt for three days and thrown in vinegar.

Pickled onions are often small, and small onions, sometimes called pearl onions, are often produced with the same seeds as large ones except planted closer together. The Chinese have a special small species for pickling, *Allium chinense*, which in China is called *jiao tou*. In Japan, where it is also popular for pickling, it is called *rakkyo*. Crystal Wax is a small variety of onion popular for pickling in the American South. It is a good thing that it pickles well, because raw, it does not keep very well in storage. In India, in Kolar and Bangalore in Karnataka state, and also in Cuddapah in Andhra Pradesh State, a small pink onion has been developed expressly for pickling.

· · ·

In 1829 Margaret Dods gave clear instructions for pickling onions:

Choose small sound silver onions, as equal in size as may be. Top and tail them. But do not pare the tops very close, as the air will soften and spoil the onions. Scald them with brine. Repeat this on the second day, and when cold, peel the onions as quickly as possible, throwing them into vinegar as they are done, to prevent their blackening. Boil vinegar enough to cover them, with sliced ginger, black and white pepper and mace; when cooled a little, pour it over the onions. Cork them well, and dip them in bottle-resin.

Some cooks peel and scald the onions, a few at a time, take them up as soon as they look transparent, and dry them in the folds of a cloth, covering them carefully to exclude the air. Some cooks scald in brine, and then parboil in milk and water. Pickled onions of the shops look beautifully white but have little *gout* [flavor].

Early in the nineteenth century, onions were pickled without peeling or trimming. They were peeled instead when served at the table and retained the strong taste of raw onion. But the taste of raw onion started fading from fashion.

This recipe is from *The Jewish Manual*, published in London in 1846:

Choose all of a size and soak in boiling brine, when cold, drain them and put them in bottles, and fill up with hot distilled vinegar; if they are to be white, use white wine vinegar; if they are to be brown, use the best distilled vinegar, adding, in both cases, a little mace, ginger, and whole pepper.

While Dods specified small onions, and it is not certain what size was to be used in *The Jewish Manual*, it is a curiosity of British pickled onions that they are often made with a medium-sized onion. The origin of this is unclear, but as far back as the eighteenth century, Hannah Glasse recommended for pickling an onion the size of a large walnut, which is larger than the usual pickling onion. The British are particularly fond of pickled onions. A standard pub lunch, the ploughman's lunch, consists of bread, cheese, salad, and pickled onions. This was probably never a lunch of ploughmen, though, since it seems to have started only in the mid-twentieth century.

In Ammerschwihr, Alsace, Pierre Gaertner pickled onions in the traditional French way. It is tarragon that makes a pickle French:

Peel the onions [small pearl type].

Wash and dry tarragon. Put some in the bottom of a pickling jar; add more tarragon and some peppercorns. Alternate layers of onions with tarragon layer on top. Cover with vinegar. Seal the jar and keep for months refrigerated.

But in Alsace there is another pickled onion tradition that Gaetner called *petits oignons à la paysanne*, country-style little onions. Note that he had his own technique against onion tears:

500 grams [a little more than a pound] pearl onions
¼ liter [1 cup] white vinegar
¼ liter [1 cup] water
1 tablespoon sugar
1 pinch salt
1 tablespoon tomato paste
1 tablespoon black peppercorns [whole], cloves [whole], and a hint of cayenne
Peel the onions. To avoid tears, place onions in a bowl of water with a little vinegar.

Put the onions in a casserole. Cover with water and vinegar. Add salt, sugar, Corinth raisins, and spices. Cook for about five minutes but in a way that the onions remain crunchy.

At the last minute add the tomato paste.

Put in a warm pickling jar and seal it. Let it cool down and then keep it for a month in the refrigerator.

Serve it cold with a wide range of foods such as meats, cold cuts and sausages, terrines, etc.

This is Pushpesh Pant's recipe for pickled onions from the northern Indian state of Punjab:

20 pearl onions
1 cup white vinegar
1 cup jaggery or soft brown sugar
1 teaspoon chili powder
1 teaspoon cumin powder
1 teaspoon Garam Masala [Indian spice blend]
6 crushed cloves garlic
salt

Put the whole onions in a large bowl, then season with salt and mix together. Put them in sterilized jars and tie cheesecloth over the top, then leave in a sunny or warm place for 2 days, shaking daily.

Open the jars and drain the onions and place them on paper towels for about 2 hours.

Put the vinegar in a deep pan, add the jaggery, all the spices, and garlic and season with salt, then bring to a boil and cook for about 10 minutes.

Add the onions and cook for a further 5–10 minutes. Remove from the heat and allow to cool overnight.

The next day put the mixture into sterilized jars, cover with cheesecloth and leave on the windowsill for a week, shaking it daily. It will be ready to eat after 7–10 days.

. . .

One of the most spectacular and simple onion dishes—and a good onion dish deserves to be as simple and unpretentious as an onion—is what the Peruvians call *encebollada*, which literally means "onioned." Onioned what? Onioned ceviche. It involves taking the national dish, ceviche, raw fish marinated in lime juice with cilantro leaves, and replacing the fish with red onions. Originally a poor people's dish, perhaps for those who could not afford fish, it is now popular throughout Peru and Ecuador.

Not only does it have the merit of being a strongly flavored, satisfying dish that is really nothing more than a bowl of onions, but it is also beautiful. The acid extracts the natural red dye from the red onions and distributes it so that the entire dish is a bright fuchsia color. It brightens the earthen color of any foods next to it or glows on the table in an earthen bowl. Looks do not disappoint. The tart flavor also enlivens the dish it accompanies.

There is a small controversy over whether the dish is Peruvian or Ecuadorean. I tend to side with Peruvian, but I can't prove it. Ceviche is Peruvian in origin, invented by a people in the north of the country, the Moche, probably in the first century. The Moche were an advanced civilization known for their pyramids and other architecture, murals, pottery, and other decorative art, and sophisticated agricultural techniques.

But the ceviche we know has been considerably Hispanicized and so, no doubt, is the encebollada as well. The Moche used fermented passion fruit juice and the Spanish introduced the use of lime, and while the Moche may have known some types of onions as other advanced South American cultures did, the use of this strain of medium-sized red onions is undoubtedly Spanish.

There is a question of whether or not to add cilantro. The fact that ceviche has cilantro, probably in part to lend color to a white dish, does not mean this colorful dish needs them. But it does add a nice dimension, and a few flecks of green can be decorative. Weighing controversies, this is my recipe for encebollada:

Slice two medium-sized peeled red onions as thin as possible. Place them in a bowl with a tablespoon of coarse salt and the juice of two limes. Mix well.

Let marinate for about twelve minutes.

Fill the bowl with lukewarm water and marinate another ten minutes.

Thoroughly drain onions and put back in an empty bowl. Add one tablespoon of coarse salt and enough lime juice to completely cover the onions (probably three or four). Add one tablespoon neutral vegetable oil such as canola or sunflower.

It will start turning red in an hour but leave overnight. Tomorrow it will be beautiful. Then finally mince a small handful of cilantro leaves [not too much; it's a mostly red dish] and toss in and mix.

Some add sugar to their encebollada. Sugar keeps turning up in onion dishes because of an urge to make onions sweeter. But these red onions are relatively sweet, and the whole point of this dish is an epic clash between two very outspoken foods—onions and limes. Let them duke it out.

. . .

An onion samba is a South African pickled onion condiment usually served with the South African meat and vegetable stew known as a *bredie*. This recipe from Cape Malay, South Africa, comes from the leading South African food writer Dorah Sitole's collection of African recipes, *Cooking from Cape to Cairo*:

Makes 1 cup

2 large onions sliced

4 tablespoons coarse salt and brown vinegar

2 tablespoons smooth apricot jam

4 tablespoons chopped coriander leaves (cilantro)

Place the onions in a bowl and sprinkle with the salt. Gently rub the salt and onion together with the fingertips to remove all bitterness from the onion juice. Wash thoroughly in a sieve to remove the salt. Return to the bowl. Mix the vinegar and apricot jam and pour over the onions. Sprinkle with coriander leaves and serve with any bredie.

. . .

Pikles (pronounced *peek-layz*) is possibly the most universal food in Haitian homes. I put the following recipe together with advice from Haitian friends:

Shred:

1 head of cabbage

3 large onions

2 carrots

Throw in a few cooked peas

Halve and add two or three habanero chilies (according to taste, but the pikles should be hot. If not, it will be what Haitians call *por blans,* which means "white people food," which is not a good thing).

Salt it thoroughly and leave for four hours. Then drain and rinse and cover with white vinegar. It will be ready in three days, but can last for months and actually improves with age.

. . .

There is probably no odder use for an onion than pickling it and tossing it into a glass of gin. The martini was originally a nineteenth-century cocktail consisting of gin and a few drops of dry vermouth. Originally the proportions were said to be 7 to 1. But then came the drier martini with even less vermouth. I do one short spray from an atomizer. In the 1958 movie *Teacher's Pet,* Gig Young suggests taking the cork from the vermouth bottle and rubbing it on the inside of the pitcher. In any event, James Bond had it completely wrong: it must be stirred not shaken. Shaking chips the ice, which dilutes the gin.

A martini is clear and colorless. In the nineteenth century bitters were sometimes added, but now it is just gin and vermouth and without a garnish looks like water. So a green olive or a strip of lemon peel is added. When a pickled onion is added, the drink becomes a Gibson. Sometimes a touch of the onion's pickle juice is added to make it more oniony.

The martini, though, seems to have been invented in California. There is a strong claim that the Gibson, like the martini, originated in San Francisco. A California bartender's guide at the turn of the twentieth century states that the Gibson was invented at the Bohemian Club in San Francisco by Charles Dana Gibson, the popular illustrator who created the "Gibson Girl." Sometimes this story is set in the venerable old Players Club on Gramercy Park in Manhattan. The story of Charles Dana Gibson inventing the Gibson seems as ubiquitous and phony as Marco Polo introducing pasta to Italy or Catherine de' Medici introducing artichokes to France. Some food stories are just loved no matter how many times they are disproved.

Charles McCabe, though a native New Yorker, was a popular columnist for the *San Francisco Chronicle* and squarely places both drinks there. His recipe for a martini was "simply splashing gin over ice, while thinking briefly of the vermouth."

McCabe claimed that his story came from Al Gibson, manager of the Crocker–Citizens Bank in Tiburon. Gibson always claimed that the cocktail came from his uncle, Walter D. K. Gibson, vice president of the Oceanic Steamship Company. A regular at the Bohemian Club, in about 1890 Walter started to complain about the bartender there. He said that he made a mediocre martini. One of his main objections, and on this he was absolutely right, was that the bartender shook martinis whereas the proper technique is to stir. He also insisted that a martini had no ingredients other than gin, vermouth, and a strip of orange peel for a garnish. So that was how the bartender made Gibson's martinis and the cocktail was called "a Gibson."

This story still leaves us wondering who added the onion. McCabe didn't know, but he did assert that Gene Baskett, a bartender in the Marina, was the first to add the pickle juice, though the onion came before that. None of the early Gibson recipes calls for an onion, or any garnish. A 1906 Boothby's Gibson recipe said "no decorations, bitters or citron fruit rind permissible." This was what distinguished it from a martini. Maybe someone couldn't stand the bareness of it.

In 1964, when stockbroker William Campbell Gibson died, his obituary in the *New York Times* reported that he claimed to have invented the Gibson at the Ritz Hotel in Paris. Of course that hotel, starting with Hemingway's claim to have liberated it in 1944, has always been a venue for questionable stories. Then there was Hugh Simons Gibson, who worked for the State Department and liked to drink with the gang at the Metropolitan Club, opened in 1863 near the White House and long a watering hole for government officials and diplomats. This Gibson liked to keep his head clear but didn't want to be the only one to have just a first drink, so he arranged with the bartender to have the rest be just water. To avoid an embarrassing mix-up, he had his bogus martinis marked with an onion garnish.

Walter D. K. Gibson's relatives lend credibility to his claim because they say he was a firm believer that onions prevented catching colds, which was a popular belief at the time. It is appealing to think that there is a martini that will keep you from catching a cold.

In 1957 revered California food writer M. F. K. Fisher wrote in *Gourmet* magazine:

> Across the Bay in The City, which is the way you talk about San Francisco if you live just outside it, people drink whatever has the quickest answer. The bleak, stylish bars off Montgomery Street are straight-faced about Gibsons, a more or less western and much ginnier version of the dry Martini, which is to say that a Gibson has almost nothing in it but cold gin, with an onion instead of an olive for the fussy oldsters.

So was the onion just for fussy oldsters? Do oldsters like pickled onions? More important, why were pickled onions available at the bar?

Personally, I don't want an onion or an olive in my martini. I'm not even sure how I feel about the vermouth, but plainly food should not be swimming around in my cocktail. Onions and olives just don't belong there. They never give you a good olive anyway. I'm okay with a piece of lemon peel, because it is purely decorative and the color is nice, but an onion barely shows itself in a glass of gin.

16

Onion Bread

According to a family myth, unproven and unprovable, as all myths should be, once, as a small child, I stole a freshly baked loaf of onion rye bread and hid under the bed and ate the whole thing. I have no memory of this event but the only part I find questionable is, why under the bed? I can still remember the smell of a freshly baked onion rye that my mother brought home from the Jewish bakery where we bought all our bread. I was an adult before I ever encountered an industrial bread. But even in that rarified world, the smell of onion rye was something special. I suppose it is my madeleine.

To make an onion rye, simply make a dough from rye flour, let it rise, roll it out to about a three-quarter-inch thickness, spread chopped onions over it, roll it up, let it rise again, and bake it.

The traditional Jewish rye was always made with large yellow Spanish onions. From the bakery's point of view, the larger the onion, the less (painful) peeling is required. But in recent years, with gourmetism a near-religion, it is sometimes suggested that red onions or sweet onions such as Vidalia or Maui Kulu are better. All those years ago, under the bed, I would never have imagined my rye bread with Hawaiian onions.

According to Karl Friedrich von Rumohr, in his 1822 *Geist der Kochkunst* ("The Essence of Cookery"), rye bread needs onions. He was writing about a dish popular throughout Europe in which bread is dissolved in broth and eaten as a kind of gruel. He wrote that in his native Germany and in many northern countries, rye bread is favored and this dish does not work well with rye because it is too bitter. The solution was to add onions, because their sweetness counteracts the bitterness of rye bread. Buttered, finely sliced, and cooked onions should be poured over finely sliced rye bread. He suggests also adding poached eggs, one for each guest. The pairing of onions and rye bread is ubiquitous, but von Rumohr offered one of the few explanations of why.

An unanswered question is why Jews have such a strong predilection for onions in their bread. It may trace back to Poland, which for centuries was Europe's great purveyor of rye flour. While it may have started with rye, it didn't stay with it.

A bialy, as every New Yorker used to know, is a small, flat, round bread with a deep well in the middle filled with onions and dusted with poppy seeds. The real name is *bialystoker kuchen*, a baked good from the eastern Polish town of Białystok—in fact the region from which one of my grandfathers came. The late food writer Mimi Sheraton went to Poland in search of authentic bialies and was told that they used to be bigger and with more poppy seeds. The onions seem to have been a constant. Immigrants from Białystok introduced them to New York in the 1920s. It is not known when bakers started making bialies in Białystok or why they had a well filled with onions. In her book *The Bialy Eaters*, published in 2000, Mimi speculated that at some point a bagel was dropped and accidentally stepped on by a heel and then the mistake was covered with onions. I cannot refute or agree with this theory.

Authentic bialies are baked with raw onions and not sautéed as some cookbooks say. Originally they were baked dark and crisp, though today they tend to be soft and light-colored.

The other great Jewish onion roll is an onion bagel, which is a very different thing. Bagels have less yeast and are not soft like a bialy. They also contain malt and sugar to give them a golden crust, unlike bialies. And the big difference is that a bagel is boiled before it is baked. The boiling gives a certain toughness of texture but it also allows these rings to keep their shape when later baked.

There is some question about the country of origin of bagels. Maybe they were not even Jewish, though onion bagels certainly were, given the Jewish onion bread tradition. A number of countries have ring-shaped breads. Italians in the city of Puglia eat *taralli*, of a similar size and shape; in Perugia and Florence they ate *ciambelle*, which were similar. In 1518, Bona Sforza from Bari in Puglia became queen of Poland. And there again is the unsupportable myth that the Italian queen comes with food, fostering the story that she introduced Poland to bagels in 1518. Records show Jewish bakers in Kraków producing *obwarzanek*, very similar to a bagel, since the early 1400s. It seems clear that bagels were Jewish and from Poland, probably originally from Kraków. It is not known when they got various toppings, but onions and poppy seeds were doubtless the first, because that is what was put on bread, especially by Jews.

This affinity for Jewish onion bread was not limited to Poland. Jews in other places also eat onions in bread. The late Edda Servi Machlin, recalling her childhood in a now-vanished Jewish community in Tuscany, reminisced about the small onion breads they called onion focaccia.

Focaccia colla Cipolla (Onion Focaccia)
Dissolve one packet of yeast in a half cup of warm water and let it sit for 5 minutes. Put four cups of unbleached flour and teaspoon of salt, the dissolved yeast, 2 soup spoons of oil. Put in a large bowl. Add 1 cup of warm water.

Place on a floured surface and knead for about 5 to 10 minutes. Shape into a bowl and place on a well-floured board in a warm place for 1 to 2 hours, until the dough doubles in volume. Punch it down and divide in 8 equal portions. Make each portion into a small ball and leave for five minutes. Flatten each with the palm of your hand to a thickness of a little less than a quarter inch.

Put one cup minced onions in a pan with 1 cup of water. Bring to a boil and cook for 2 or 3 minutes. Drain well and put two soup spoons of onions on each focaccia. Sprinkle with coarse salt and black pepper and oil.

Heat the oven to 500 degrees F. Place the focaccia and bake for 8 to 10 minutes on well-oiled and floured boards [or baking sheets].

Onion bread is not uniquely Jewish. The Scots, who enjoy milk rolls that they call "baps," often make onion baps. Here is an onion bread from American priest turned chef Robert Farrar Capon, published in his 1969 book, *The Supper of the Lamb*. The onions are scalded in milk but not sautéed:

2 cups milk (or part water)
1 tablespoon butter
2 teaspoons salt
2 tablespoons sugar
4 tablespoons yeast
¼ cup lukewarm water
1 teaspoon sugar
6 cups sifted flour (approximately)
Scald the milk in a large (6 quarts) pan. Add the next 3 ingredients. Cool to lukewarm.

Combine the yeast, water, and 1 teaspoon of sugar in a small bowl and let stand while the milk mixture is cooking.

Scald 1 cup minced onion with milk. Add to yeast mixture, beat in 1 egg.

Sift ⅓ of the flour into the cooled milk mixture, and continue beating in flour until you have a moderately stiff dough. Turn this out onto a floured board and knead for 5 minutes until glossy.

Return the dough to the same pot you scalded the milk in (but washed, dried, and buttered), cover with a damp towel, and let rise until doubled in bulk.

Divide the dough in half and each in three. Shape each piece into a long rope. Make two braided loaves. Put these in buttered loaf pans, let rise, brush with milk or beaten egg white. Sprinkle with some chopped onion. Bake at 350 degrees F.

In eighteenth-century New England, onion shortcake was popular. Shortcake is basically a sweet biscuit made with flour, sugar, butter, and baking soda. In the American South, corn bread is sometimes baked with onions. This recipe for corn bread "lace" cakes is from Evelyn Rogers in *Sweet Vidalia Onions*. Lace cakes are made with thin batter so it spreads on the griddle, but the recipe can also be used to make the thicker onion corn bread known as griddle cakes. Griddle cakes are an old way of baking derived from cultures such as the ancient Celtic where there were no ovens.

1 cup plain meal
1 ¼ cups water
½ teaspoon salt
1 cup sweet [Vidalia or Vidalia-type] onions, finely chopped
Vegetable oil
Grease heavy griddle with one teaspoon of oil. Heat griddle over medium heat. It is hot enough when a drop of water

sizzles on it. The batter should be thin for lace cakes but a little thicker for heavy cornbread cakes. Cook about 3 minutes on each side or until golden brown. Cakes are great served with vegetables.

Maybe, but I don't think a bread is worth crawling under the bed to eat unless it has lots of onions. Our senses guide us to what is right and what is wrong in food. A blueberry bagel is clearly wrong, but onion and bread is just right.

17

Sandwiches

James Beard once wrote, "I can easily make a whole meal of onion sandwiches, for me they are one of the greatest treats I know." According to legend, Beard built his name on an onion sandwich. Irma Rhode and her brother Bill were famous for hors d'oeuvre recipes, one of which was a slice of onion on a piece of brioche. Most great food writers from Apicius to Hannah Glasse to Beard lifted recipes from others, and so Beard, a little-known caterer, got a great deal of attention when he published his onion sandwich recipe, which was a slice of onion on a buttery brioche.

Even if this story is apocryphal, it is true that to Beard an onion sandwich was a great meal. To the Romans, a slice of onion between two slices of bread was a good breakfast. To the British poor, an onion sandwich was basic sustenance.

Ernest Hemingway, who grew up eating onion sandwiches in suburban Chicago of wild onion fame, was a prominent onion fan. Hemingway's father, a doctor and a great outdoorsman, taught Hemingway how to find wild onions and put them in a sandwich. To Hemingway, an onion sandwich was the perfect lunch while out fishing. He liked a slice of onion on bread with peanut butter. In *Islands in the Stream*, the sandwich is referred to as the "Mount Everest Special" because it is "one of the highest points in the sandwich-makers' art." Try it if you want, but I'm not recommending it.

In Vidalia, Georgia, a slice of the local sweet onion is de rigueur on a cheeseburger, sometimes with another raw slice as a garnish on the side.

The 1950 movie *Harvey*, starring James Stewart as a man who befriends an imaginary six-foot rabbit, started people thinking about egg and onion sandwiches. The movie is based on a Broadway hit play that makes no mention of egg and onion sandwiches. But the movie, written by Mary Chase, who also wrote the play, along with Hollywood writers Oscar Brodney and Myles Connolly, adds an egg and onion sandwich scene.

The character Myrtle suggests coffee to Wilson and a ham and rye sandwich, a reliable standard. Then she gets a little bolder and suggests an egg and onion sandwich. "I'd love to make you one," Myrtle insists. "The egg and onions are waiting in the kitchen." Wilson goes with the egg and onion and seems to know what to expect, though we don't, because this is not standard fare.

Off they go and later it is clear that they have bonded over egg and onion. The way she seductively says that the eggs and onions are waiting seems to imply a simple dish, but we can't be sure. Audiences have been speculating ever since. Some have suggested that the sandwich contains just sautéed chopped onions and scrambled eggs. A more interesting possibility is a slice of onion wilted in hot butter with an egg fried on top and then placed on a roll. Perhaps too sloppy for a first date, though.

In Ireland, where egg and onion sandwiches are popular, this usually means an egg salad sandwich with thinly sliced green onions. Back in the United States, President Calvin Coolidge liked his egg and onion sandwich made with egg salad too. His was a kind of oniony egg salad sandwich on rye bread, with one chopped sweet onion mixed with three hard-boiled eggs, mayonnaise, a little dry mustard powder, salt, and pepper.

James Beard, who had a great fondness for egg and onion sandwiches, made his with hard-boiled eggs:

> Sautée ½ cup finely chopped onion or green onion in one tablespoon of butter for a few minutes until wilted and soft. Toss in about ½ cup finely chopped mushrooms, if you have them, and cook down with the onions for two or three minutes. Salt and pepper the mixture, let it cool, then toss with four finely chopped hard boiled eggs and, if it needs binding, a tiny bit of mayonnaise. Spread on whole wheat or rye bread and there's your sandwich.

Beard also made an onion sandwich:

For this I have found there is nothing better than oatmeal bread. Spread it with butter, top with paper thin onion slices, salt, clap the other slice of bread on top and press down tightly.

To get only slightly more elaborate he suggested one of his favorites:

Homemade bread, well buttered, spread with mashed sardines, a few drops of lemon juice, and a thin slice of onion, eaten with a glass of beer or wine.

To make great onion sandwiches Beard gave this recipe for oatmeal bread:

Dissolve 2 packages active dry yeast and 2 teaspoons sugar in 1 cup lukewarm water—110 to 115 degrees. Let stand for ten minutes, then stir very well. Cream ⅓ cup butter in a large mixing bowl, add 1 cup boiling water, and stir until completely melted. Add 1 cup rolled oats, ⅓ cup molasses, and 1 tablespoon salt. Blend thoroughly and cool to lukewarm. Add the yeast, then fold in 5½ cups sifted flour. Add 1 egg and beat well. Put the dough in a buttered mixing bowl, turning it so it is well-greased on all sides, then refrigerate for at least two hours—you can leave it for 3 or 4 hours and it won't hurt. Turn out the chilled dough on a floured board and shape into two loaves. Place in well-buttered 9 by 5 inch loaf pans, and let rise in a warm, draft free spot until double in bulk, about 2 hours.

Bake in a 350 degree oven for approximately 1 hour, or until the loaves are nicely browned and sound hollow when you rap the bottom with your knuckles. Remove from the pans and cool on a rack. This makes excellent sandwiches and the best toast ever.

For some, an onion sandwich is the simplest of concoctions. The writer Joseph Mitchell said of the proprietor of McSorley's, the venerable Irish saloon in New York City, "He liked to get a whole onion in the hollowed out heel of a loaf of French bread and eat it as if it were an apple."

You have to choose from among the great ideas of others. I like the sloppy version (sloppy is always good when it comes to food) with the fried egg, and I would take Beard's advice, often excellent advice to follow, about the oatmeal bread. And the combination of sardines and raw onions is irresistible. Irresistible is the goal of a great recipe. I'll leave the peanut butter to Hemingway.

ACKNOWLEDGMENTS

Thank you to Nancy Miller, my long-time editor, for working so hard and with such dedication, and to Charlotte Sheedy, my agent, friend, and supporter. Thanks to my friend for so many years Victor Higon-Torres for help on Catalonia, my dear friend Sylvia Plachy for insights into Hungarian food tradition and as always her wonderful portrait of myself and Zola the cat, Jaideep Hardikar for sharing his great knowledge of Indian onion politics, and Alana Buddingh for her help from Hawaii and for first telling me about Maui onions. How lucky I am to have such friends. Also thanks to Robin Shimanuki at the University of Hawaii and Bob Stafford at the Vidalia Onion Committee.

BIBLIOGRAPHY

Achaya, K. T. *A Historical Dictionary of Indian Food.* Mumbai: Oxford University Press, 1998.

Aguilera, César. *Historia de la alimentación Mediterránea.* Madrid: Editorial Complutense, 1997.

Algar, Ayla. *Classical Turkish Cooking.* New York: HarperCollins, 1991.

Anderson, E. N. *The Food of China.* New Haven: Yale University Press, 1988.

Artusi, Pellegrino. *La scienza in cucina e l'arte di mangiar bene.* Milan: Sperling & Kupfer, 1891.

Balinska, Maria. *The Bagel: The Surprising History of a Modest Bread.* New Haven: Yale University Press, 2008.

Baron, Robert C., ed. *The Garden and Farm Books of Thomas Jefferson.* Golden, CO: Fulcrum, 1987.

Beard, James. *Beard on Food.* New York: Alfred A. Knopf, 1974.

Beeton, Isabella. *The Book of Household Management.* London: S. O. Beeton, 1861.

Bienvenu, Marcelle, ed. *The Picayune's Creole Cook Book: Sesquicentennial Edition.* New Orleans: Times-Picayune, 1987; first published in 1901.

Block, Eric. *Garlic and Other Alliums: The Lore and the Science.* Cambridge, UK: Royal Society of Chemistry, 2010.

Blot, Pierre. *Hand-Book of Practical Cookery, For Ladies and Professional Cooks: Containing the Whole Science and Art of Preparing Human Food.* New York: D. Appleton, 1867.

Bode, W. K. H. *European Gastronomy: The Story of Man's Food and Eating Customs.* London: Hodder and Stoughton, 1994.

Bon, Alejandro. *Leonor, cocinera superior.* Barcelona: José Montesó, 1946.

Boni, Ada. *Il talismano della felicità.* Rome: Casa Editrice Colombo, 1997; first published in 1929.

———. *La cucina romana.* Rome: Newton Compton Editori, 1998.

Brears, Peter. *Cooking & Dining in Medieval England.* Totnes, UK: Prospect, 2012.

———. *Tudor Cookery: Recipes and History.* Swindon, UK: English Heritage, 2003.

Brenan, Gerald. *South from Granada.* New York: Farrar, Straus and Cudahy, 1957.

Briggs, Margaret. *Garlic & Onions: The Many Uses & Medicinal Benefits.* Leicester, UK: Abbeydale Press, 2007.

Busca Isusi, José Maria. *Antología gastronómica de José Maria Busca Isusi.* Hondarribia, Spain: Academia Vasca de Gastronomía, n.d. (based on articles in *El Diario Vasco*, 1983–86).

———. *Traditional Basque Cooking.* Reno: University of Nevada Press, 1987.

Calderbank, Daniel A., Bill Rodger, and Jim Kirkness. *Growing Onions & Shallots.* Bolton, UK: Ross Anderson, 1986.

Capon, Robert Farrar. *The Supper of the Lamb: A Culinary Reflection.* New York: Modern Library, 2002; first published in 1969.

Castelvetro, Giacomo. *Brieve racconto di tutte le radici, di tutte l'erbe e di tutti i frutti, che crudi o cotti in Italia si mangiano.* First published in 1614. Translated by Gillian Riley as *The Fruit, Herbs & Vegetables of Italy.* London: Viking, 1989.

Chadwick, Mrs. J. *Home Cookery: A Collection of Tried Receipts both Foreign and Domestic.* Boston: Crosby, Nichols, 1853.

Chamberlain, Samuel. *Clémentine in the Kitchen.* New York: Modern Library, 2001.

Chang, K. C. *Food in Chinese Culture: Anthropological and Historical Perspectives.* New Haven: Yale University Press, 1977.

Charpentier, Henri, and Boyden Sparkes. *Those Rich and Great Ones, or Life à la Henri.* London: Victor Gollancz, 1935.

Child, Lydia Maria Francis. *The American Frugal Housewife,* 12th edition. Boston: Carter, Hendee, 1833; first published in 1828.

Christian Woman's Exchange of New Orleans. *Creole Cookery.* New Orleans: T. H. Thomason, 1885.

Correnti, Pino. *Il libro d'oro della cucina e dei vini di Sicilia.* Milan: Mursia, 1976.

Crossley-Holland, Kevin. *The Exeter Book Riddles.* New York: Penguin, 1993.

Custer, Elizabeth Bacon. *Boots & Saddles*. Middletown, DE: Big Byte Books, 2020.

Davidson, Alan, ed. *The Oxford Companion to Food*. Oxford: Oxford University Press, 1999.

de la Falaise, Maxime. *Seven Centuries of English Cooking*. New York: Grove Press, 1973.

Diat, Louis. *Cooking a la Ritz*. New York: J. B. Lippincott, 1941.

Dods, Margaret. *The Cook and Housewife's Manual*. London: Rosters, 1829.

Dumas, Alexandre. *Grand dictionnaire de cuisine*. Paris: UGE Éditions 10/18, 1998; first published in 1873.

Ellis, William. *The Country Housewife's Family Companion*. Totnes, UK: Prospect, 2000; first published in 1750.

Escoffier, Auguste. *Le guide culinaire*. Paris: Flammarion, 1921.

Estes, Rufus. *Good Things to Eat: As Suggested by Rufus*. Jenks, OK: Howling at the Moon, 1999; originally self-published in 1911.

Evelyn, John. *Acetaria: A Discourse of Sallets*. Totnes, UK: Prospect, 1996; first published in 1699.

Farmer, Fannie Merritt. *The Boston Cooking-School Cookbook*. Boston, 1896.

Fisher, M. F. K. *The Art of Eating*. New York: Macmillan, 1990.

FitzGibbon, Theodora. *A Taste of Ireland*. London: Barnes & Noble, 1994.

Folse, John D. *The Encyclopedia of Cajun & Creole Cuisine.* Gonzales, LA: Chef John Folse, 2006.

Frolov, Wanda L. *Katish: Our Russian Cook.* New York: Modern Library, 2001; first published in 1947.

Gaertner, Pierre, and Robert Frédérick. *La cuisine alsacienne.* Paris: Flammarion, 1979.

García Rivas, Heriberto. *Cocina prehispánica mexicana.* Mexico City: Panorama Editorial, 2001.

Giacosa, Ilaria Gozzini. *A Taste of Ancient Rome.* Translated by Anna Herklotz. Chicago: University of Chicago Press, 1992.

Glasse, Hannah. *The Art of Cookery Made Plain and Easy.* Facsimile of 1747 edition. Totnes, UK: Prospect, 1995.

Glover, Brian. *Onion: The Essential Cook's Guide to Onions, Garlic, Leeks, Spring Onions, Shallots and Chives.* London: Lorenz Books, 2001.

Greenberg, Joel. *A Natural History of the Chicago Region.* Chicago: University of Chicago Press, 2002.

Greiner, Tuisco. *The New Onion Culture.* New York: Orange Judd, 1903.

Griffith, Linda, and Fred Griffith. *Onions, Onions, Onions: Delicious Recipes for the World's Favorite Secret Ingredient.* Shelburne, VT: Chapters, 1994.

Grigson, Jane. *English Food.* London: Penguin, 1993; first published in 1974.

———. *Jane Grigson's Vegetable Book.* London: Penguin, 1980.

Hagen, Ann. *A Second Handbook of Anglo-Saxon Food & Drink: Production & Distribution*. Norfolk, UK: Anglo Saxon Books, 1995.

Harland, Marion. *Common Sense in the Household: A Manual of Practical Housewifery*. New York: Charles Scribner's Sons, 1871.

Hastrop, Kate. *Know Your Onions*. Feltham, UK: Hamlyn Paperbacks, 1980.

Hieatt, Constance B., ed. *An Ordinance of Pottage: An Edition of the Fifteenth Century Culinary Recipes in Yale University's MS Beinecke 163*. London: Prospect Books, 1988.

Hill, Annabella P. *Mrs. Hill's Southern Practical Cookery and Receipt Book*. Columbia, SC: University of South Carolina, 1995; first published in 1867, revised 1872.

Hope, Annette. *A Caledonian Feast*. London: Grafton, 1989.

Hope, Rose-Ellen. "The Legacy of Western Camas." In *The Wilder Shores of Gastronomy: Twenty Years of the Best Food Writing from the Journal* "Petits Propos Culinaires," edited by Alan Davidson. Berkeley: Ten Speed, 2002.

Horváth, Ilona. *Szakácskönyv*. Budapest: Kiadó, 1993.

Howard, Maria Willett. *Lowney's Cook Book*. Boston: Walter M. Lowney, 1912.

Huici Miranda, Ambrosio. *La cocina hispano-magrebí durante la época almohade*. Gijón, Spain: Ediciones Trea, 2005.

Ignacio Taibo I, Paco. *Encuentro de dos fogones*. Mexico City: Promoción y Imagen, 1992.

Irwin, Florence. *The Cookin' Woman: Irish Country Recipes*. Belfast: Blackstaff Press, 1986; first published in 1949.

Jones, Henry A., and Louis K. Mann. *Onions and Their Allies*. New York: Interscience Publishers, 1963.

Kiple, Kenneth F., and Kriemhild Coneè Ornelas, eds. *The Cambridge World History of Food*, Vol. 1. Cambridge: Cambridge University Press, 2000.

Koehler, Jeff. *Morocco: A Culinary Journey with Recipes from the Spice-Scented Markets of Marrakech to the Date-Filled Oasis of Zagora*. San Francisco: Chronicle, 2012.

Krondl, Michael. *Around the American Table: Treasured Recipes and Food Traditions from the American Cookery Collection of the New York Public Library*. Holbrook, MA: Adams MediaCorp, 1995.

Kumar, Vijaya. *The Secret Benefits of Onion and Garlic*. New Delhi: Sterling, 2006.

Kurlansky, Mark. *Milk!: A 10,000-Year Food Fracas*. New York: Bloomsbury, 2018.

La Cerva, Gina Rae. *Feasting Wild: In Search of the Last Untamed Food*. Vancouver: Greystone Books, 2020.

Lang, George. *The Cuisine of Hungary*. New York: Atheneum, 1985.

Lapitz, Juan José. *La cocina de Shishito en la Belle Epoque*. Hondarribia, Spain: Baroja, 1990.

Lassen, Agnete W., Eckart Frahm, and Klaus Wagensonner, eds. *Ancient Mesopotamia Speaks: Highlights of the Yale Babylonia Collection*. New Haven: Yale University Press, 2019.

Laughlin, Harry Hamilton. *Duration of the Several Mitotic Stages in the Dividing Root-Tip Cells of the Common Onion*. Washington, DC: Carnegie Institution, 1919.

Lebey, Claude, project director. *Bretagne: Produits du terroir et recettes traditionnelles (L'inventaire du patrimoine culinaire de la France).* Paris: Albin Michel / Conseil National des Arts Culinaires, 1994.

Le ménagier de Paris. Edited by Georgine E. Brereton and Janet M. Ferrier. Oxford: Oxford University Press, 1981; first published in 1393. See also *Le mesnagier de Paris* (1393), translated into modern French by Karin Veltschi. Paris: Le Livre de Poche, 1994.

Leslie, Eliza. *Miss Leslie's Directions for Cookery: An Unabridged Reprint of the 1851 Classic.* Mineola, NY: Dover, 1999.

MacDonogh, Giles. *A Palate in Revolution: Grimod de La Reynière and the Almanach des Gourmands.* London: Robin Clark, 1987.

Machlin, Edda Servi. *Classic Cuisine of the Italian Jews.* New York: Dodd Mead, 1984.

Mackie, Cristine. *Life and Food in the Caribbean.* Kingston, Jamaica: Ian Randle, 1995.

Mariani, John. *The Dictionary of American Food & Drink.* New York: Ticknor and Fields, 1983.

Marshall, Agnes Bertha. *Mrs. A. B. Marshall's Cookery Book.* London: Ward, Lock, 1887.

Mason, Laura, and Catherine Brown. *The Taste of Britain.* London: Harper, 2006.

May, Robert. *The Accomplisht Cook, or the Art and Mystery of Cookery.* Totnes, UK: Prospect, 1994; first published in 1665.

McCabe, Charles. *The Good Man's Weakness.* San Francisco: Chronicle, 1974.

McGee, Harold. *On Food and Cooking: The Science and Lore of the Kitchen.* New York: Charles Scribner's Sons, 1984.

Médecin, Jacques. *La cuisine du comté de Nice.* Paris: Julliard, 1972.

Millet-Robinet, Cora. *Maison rustique des dames.* First published in 1844. Translated by Tom Jaine as *The French Country Housewife.* London: Prospect, 2017.

Montefiore, Lady Judith Cohen. *The Jewish Manual: Practical Information in Jewish and Modern Cookery.* First published in 1846. Introduction to the modern edition by Raphael Chaim. New York: Nightingale Books, 1983.

Moon, Rosemary. *Onions, Onions, Onions: Globe, Spanish, Vidalia, Walla Walla, Shallot and More.* Buffalo: Firefly, 2000.

Pant, Pushpesh. *India Cookbook.* London: Phaidon, 2010.

Pardo Bazán, Emilia. *La cocina española antigua.* Madrid: Sociedad Anónima Renacimiento, 1913.

Parienté, Henriette, and Geneviève de Ternant. *Histoire de la cuisine française.* Paris: Éditions de la Martinière, 1994.

Peterson, T. Sarah. *Acquired Taste: The French Origins of Modern Cooking.* Ithaca, NY: Cornell University Press, 1994.

Pizer, Vernon. *Eat the Grapes Downward: An Uninhibited Romp through the Surprising World of Food.* New York: Dodd, Mead, 1983.

Platina: On Right Pleasure and Good Health. Translated by Mary Ella Milham. Tempe, AZ: Medieval & Renaissance Texts & Studies, 1998; first published in 1465.

Pliny: Natural History: Vol. VI, Books XX–XXIII. Translated by W. H. S. Jones. Cambridge, MA: Harvard University Press, 1964.

Porterfield, James D. *Dining by Rail: The History and Recipes of America's Golden Age of Railroad Cuisine.* New York: St. Martin's Griffin, 1993.

Prudhomme, Paul. *Chef Paul Prudhomme's Louisiana Kitchen.* New York: William Morrow, 1984.

Rawlings, Marjorie Kinnan. *Cross Creek Cookery.* New York: Fireside, 1996; first published in 1942.

Reboul, Jean-Baptiste. *La cuisinière provençale.* Marseille: Tacussel, 1897.

Roberts, Jonathan. *The Origins of Fruit and Vegetables.* New York: Universe, 2001.

Rodinson, Maxime, A. J. Arberry, and Charles Perry. *Medieval Arab Cookery.* Totnes, UK: Prospect, 2001.

Rogers, Evelyn. *Sweet Vidalia Onions: Blue Ribbon Recipes.* Vidalia, GA: Evelyn Rogers, 1986.

Root, Waverley. *Food.* New York: Simon & Schuster, 1980.

———. *The Food of France.* New York: Vintage, 1992.

Sahni, Julie. *Classic Indian Cooking.* New York: William Morrow, 1980.

Santos, Barbara. *The Maui Onion Cookbook.* Berkeley: Celestial Arts, 1996.

Scully, D. Eleanor, and Terrence Scully. *Early French Cookery: Sources, History, Original Recipes and Modern Adaptations.* Ann Arbor: University of Michigan Press, 1995.

Scully, Terrence, ed. and trans. *Chiquart's "On Cookery."* New York: Peter Lang, 1986.

Senderens, Alain. *The Table Beckons.* New York: Farrar, Straus and Giroux, 1993.

Sheraton, Mimi. *The Bialy Eaters: The Story of a Bread and a Lost World.* New York: Broadway Books, 2000.

———. *1,000 Foods to Eat Before You Die.* New York: Workman, 2015.

Simeti, Mary Taylor. *Pomp and Sustenance: Twenty-five Centuries of Sicilian Food.* New York: Alfred A. Knopf, 1989.

Simmons, Amelia. *American Cookery.* Hartford, CT: Hudson & Goodwin, 1796.

Simoons, Frederick J. *Eat Not This Flesh: Food Avoidances from Prehistory to the Present.* Madison: University of Wisconsin Press, 1994.

———. *Food in China: A Cultural and Historical Inquiry.* Boca Raton, FL: CRC Press, 1991.

Sitole, Dorah. *Cooking from Cape to Cairo.* Cape Town: Tafelberg, 2009.

Soyer, Alexis. *The Pantropheon, or A History of Food and Its Preparation in Ancient Times.* New York: Paddington Press, 1977; first published in 1853.

———. *Soyer's Shilling Cookery for the People.* London: Routledge, Warne and Routledge, 1854.

Spencer, Colin. *British Food: An Extraordinary Thousand Years of History.* New York: Columbia University Press, 2003.

Terrail, Claude. *Ma Tour d'Argent.* Paris: Marabout, 1975.

Tickletooth, Tabitha. *The Dinner Question, or How to Dine Well and Economically*. London: Routledge, Warne and Routledge, 1860.

Toomre, Joyce, trans. *Classic Russian Cooking: Elena Molokhovets' "A Gift to Young Housewives."* Bloomington: Indiana University Press, 1992.

Trager, James. *The Food Chronology*. New York: Henry Holt, 1995.

Tschirky, Oscar. *The Cook Book by "Oscar" of the Waldorf*. Akron, OH: Werner, 1896.

Tsuji, Shizuo. *Japanese Cooking: A Simple Art*. New York: Kodansha, 1980.

Valentine, Nancy. *All About Bermuda Onions: How to Cook Onions, Their History & Health Benefits*. Bermuda: Island Press, 1991.

Vehling, Joseph Dommers, ed. and trans. *Apicius: Cookery and Dining in Imperial Rome*. New York: Dover, 1977.

Verdon, René. *The White House Chef Cookbook*. New York: Doubleday, 1967.

Verrall, William. *William Verrall's Cookery Book 1759*. Lewes, UK: Southover Press, 1999.

Vieira, Edite. *The Taste of Portugal*. London: Grub Street, 1995.

Visser, Margaret. *Much Depends on Dinner*. New York: Collier, 1986.

von Rumohr, Karl Friedrich. *Geist der Kochkunst*. First published in 1822. Translated by Barbara Yeomans as *The Essence of Cookery*. London: Prospect, 1993.

Welsch, Roger L., and Linda K. Welsch. *Cather's Kitchens: Foodways in Literature and Life*. Lincoln: University of Nebraska Press, 1987.

Williams, R. Omosunlola. *Miss Williams' Cookery Book.* London: Longmans, Green, 1957.

Wolfert, Paula. *Couscous and Other Good Food from Morocco.* New York: Harper & Row, 1973.

Wolke, Robert L. *What Einstein Told His Cook 2: The Sequel.* New York: W. W. Norton, 2005.

Wondrich, David. *Imbibe!* New York: Perigee, 2007.

Wright, Clifford A. *Cucina Paradiso: The Heavenly Food of Sicily.* New York: Simon & Schuster, 1992.

ARTICLES

Aggie Horticulture. "The Onion That Came to Texas but Never Left the Same." Texas A&M Agrilife Extension. https://aggie-hort.tamu .edu/archives/parsons/publications/onions/ONIONHIS.html.

Biswas, Parthasarathi. *Indian Express.* "Explained: What Is Driving Onion Prices." September 2, 2020. https://indianexpress.com/article /explained/simply-put-what-is-driving-onion-prices-6124556/.

Block, Eric. "The Chemistry of Garlic and Onions." *Scientific American* 252, no. 3 (March 1985).

Gettleman, Jeffrey, Julfikar Ali Manik, and Suhasini Raj. "India Isn't Letting a Single Onion Leave the Country." *New York Times,* October 1, 2019.

The Hindu. "The Political Price of Onions," December 25, 2010 (updated November 17, 2021). https://www.thehindu.com/opinion/editorial /The-political-price-of-onions/article15607000.ece.

LIST OF ILLUSTRATIONS

INDEX

Note: Page numbers in *italics* refer to photographs.

A NOTE ON THE AUTHOR

MARK KURLANSKY is the *New York Times* bestselling author of *The Unreasonable Virtue of Fly Fishing, Milk!, Havana, Paper, The Big Oyster, 1968, Salt, The Basque History of the World, Cod,* and *Salmon,* among other titles. He has received the Dayton Literary Peace Prize, *Bon Appétit*'s Food Writer of the Year Award, the James Beard Award, and the Glenfiddich Award. He lives in New York City.

www.markkurlansky.com